HOTEL LIFE

HOTEL LIFE

BY

NORMAN S. HAYNER
ASSOCIATE PROFESSOR OF SOCIOLOGY
UNIVERSITY OF WASHINGTON

Chapel Hill
The University of North Carolina Press
1936

MANUFACTURED IN THE UNITED STATES OF AMERICA

THIS BOOK WAS DIGITALLY PRINTED.

To
UNA MIDDLETON HAYNER
Fellow Tourist

ACKNOWLEDGMENTS

SOME OF the material used in this book has been published elsewhere. For permission to use it the author wishes to thank the editors of the *American Journal of Sociology, Sociology and Social Research, The Survey* and *Social Forces*.

The writer is under obligation to many hotel men who have granted long interviews and to numerous students and hotel dwellers who have written interesting papers. Unfortunately the use of names might identify confidential material. He is particularly indebted to Professor Jesse F. Steiner, University of Washington, and to Mr. W. I. Hamilton, personnel director of the Waldorf-Astoria in New York, who read and criticized the manuscript; to Professor Robert E. Park, University of Chicago, who encouraged the project with many helpful suggestions; and to Una Middleton Hayner, whose painstaking editorial assistance and numerous constructive criticisms have been a constant source of inspiration.

NORMAN S. HAYNER

University of Washington
Seattle
November, 1935

CONTENTS

HOTEL LIFE

CHAPTER I

HOTEL LIFE AND PERSONALITY

IN THE metropolitan hotel the guest is only a number. His mark of identification is a key. His status, in so far as he has any, is almost entirely a matter of outward appearance and "front." The bellboy and waiter judge the visitor largely by the size of tip he is likely to yield. Even the barbers look at him in a cold, hungry, calculating way. His relation to the host is completely depersonalized. The personal hospitable contact between landlord and guest in the inns and taverns of the past has been replaced by impersonality and standardized correctness. The huge hostelries of our great cities have all the comforts and luxuries that science can devise, but they have lost, as have many other institutions, the friendly individuality of an earlier day.

The modern hotel dweller is characteristically detached in his interests from the place in which he sleeps. Although physically near the other guests he is socially distant. He meets his neighbors, perhaps, but does not know them. He "may become ill and die without producing a ripple on the surface of the common life. He loses his identity as if a numbered patient in a hospital or a criminal in a prison."[1]

But the human being is like a vine. He is made to have attachments and to tie onto things. If the tendrils are broken it is a great loss. Hotel dwellers have, to a large extent, broken these attachments not only to things and to places, but to other people. They are free, it is true, but they are

---

[1] From the unpublished hotel experience of a woman who had lived for brief periods in about five hundred hotels. Hereafter, unless otherwise indicated, all such quotations and excerpts are unpublished material.

often restless and unhappy. "At home I should have felt relaxed and happy—here I am always restless unless quite exhausted."[2]

I have traveled a good deal but never learned to enjoy life in a hotel. I recall when I was a boy sitting on the balcony of the old Merchant's Hotel in St. Paul enjoying a delightful sense of utter loneliness, watching the crowd pass by on the pavement and reflecting how utterly indifferent they were to all my joys and sorrows. I felt so badly about it that I wept.

I have never got over this feeling of utter loneliness, whenever I have been condemned to live for any length of time in a hotel. I am always timid and self-conscious when I enter a hotel and feel myself assessed and tagged and chucked away in one of its luxurious cells.

I think American hotels are much the worst in the world. In Europe, entering a small hotel, you really felt that you were welcome. You frequently got acquainted with the proprietor, but I have never had that experience in America.

I do not remember ever having made an acquaintance in an American hotel. I wasn't looking for companionship, to be sure, and certainly would not have encouraged the casual advances of any stranger I happened to meet. But it was not so abroad. I remember making the acquaintance of a little Jewish woman from South Africa in a Swiss hotel. We took long walks together and became quite well acquainted in spite of the fact that conversations were carried on in German. The smaller residential hotels abroad have somewhat the character of a club. You rather expect to meet interesting people there but it is not so in America, as far as my experience goes.[3]

The anonymity and impersonality that make the hotel "the most lonely place in the world" also make it free. So long as the guest preserves the conventions he may do as he pleases and no one will object. Among the many occupational types that enjoy this freedom is the school teacher.

---

[2] From a manuscript written by a young woman.

[3] From the hotel experience of a university professor.

After the day's struggles with Mary and Johnny she finds escape in the soothing quiet of her skyscraper haven. Especially is this true in the West where there is not the stigma attached to hotel life for young women that persists in the East. In a hotel the lights are always on if she comes home late, and no one will ask questions; she can sleep late Saturday morning without being disturbed by children drumming on the piano; the water is always hot; there is an abundance of linen; the room is always warm—life is luxuriantly comfortable. The young woman cited above disliked the hotel when she first came, but at the end of four months, in spite of a protesting conscience, she liked it—the idleness, the heat, the comfort, the "cushy" life.

I do not know of any place where one feels more independent. If a person wishes to dine one night at 7 : 30 o'clock and the next at 5 : 30, nobody is inconvenienced; if he wishes to sleep late or catch an early train, it disarranges no one. Too much of this freedom makes one selfish and inconsiderate of the rights of others.

But if one is tired there is no place where one can more completely relax than in a hotel. The main disadvantage is that a person has little chance to show any originality in selecting his surroundings. One hotel bedroom is very like another; meals are surprisingly uniform even when chosen from an *a la carte* menu; there is no friendly, intimate method of entertaining one's friends; and one is very much in the public eye.[4]

Hotel men say, "Hotels should be more homelike," and they slip a newspaper under the door with the compliments of the management. Advertisements almost universally tell how "homelike" it is at the Grand Hotel. "The nearer the hotel can approach the home itself," wrote the manager of Chicago's Blackstone in an article, "the more it appeals to the better class of discriminating American travelers." But as Sinclair Lewis points out in *Work of Art*, "a fair number

---

[4] From a paper by a traveling librarian.

of guests might be so earnestly sick of wives, yelping children, solicitous mothers-in-law, balky furnaces, household
bills, trouble with cooks, and getting the lawn mowed that
the one reason why they came to hotels at all was to get
away from feeling at home."[5]

Some people prefer the intimacy of the small establishment,
where everyone calls the traveler by name, and theoretically,
at least, he is made to feel "at home." Sometimes, however, the
traveler doesn't want to feel at home. He wants to feel as far
away from home as possible. He should go to one of the big
hotels. In these great barracks, one lives in comfort, no one
speaks, and one's comings and goings are unobserved. This
might pall after a time, but it is a great vacation for a short
while.[6]

Living in hotels for a long time may be a very lonesome
existence. "With life going on all about him and everyone
seemingly so busy, with no thought of the other fellow, one
can get so discouraged and desolate that most anything
could happen."[7] Cities like San Francisco and Seattle, that
lead the country in the number of full-time hotel guest
rooms in proportion to their populations also tend to rank
high in the incidence of suicide. Studies have shown that
the "suicide locale," i.e., the area having the highest rate
for self-destruction, in the large American city, not only includes the lodging house district, but also the neighborhood
of better-class hotels.[8] Self-murder is sometimes the tragic
climax of the demoralizing lonesomeness that often accom-
panies mobility and detachment.

Like a traveler in a foreign country the hotel dweller rarely

---

[5] Pp. 259-60.

[6] Adapted from H. V. Obrien in the *Chicago Daily News* as quoted by the
Hotel Monthly, June 1933, p. 43.

[7] The observation of a ballet dancer.

[8] See Calvin Schmid, "Suicide in Minneapolis," *American Journal of Sociology*, XXXIX (July 1933), 31, 34 and 45; also Ruth Schonle Cavan, *Suicide*
(Chicago, 1928), chap. V, "Suicide in America's Second City."

has roots in the local community. He is notoriously difficult to interest in such activities as filling out census blanks or supporting the Community Fund. As indicated by the percentage of non-voting, "the guests in Chicago's outlying residential hotels were not as civic-minded as the house and apartment dwellers in the same neighborhoods."[9] This detachment from any sense of responsibility for community enterprises occasionally makes a news story.

Apathy of hotel and apartment guests toward the census count of Seattle's population is approaching alarming proportions. Reports of discouraged enumerators who have made, in instances, as many as eight and ten trips to such hostelries only to find the census slips have been ignored, aroused Supervisor L. A. (Bill) Williams to action today.

The trouble is that many people—especially young couples— residing in hotels and apartment houses do not care whether they are counted or not. [Said Mr. Williams.] In numerous cases they have frankly said so when urged by house managers or clerks to fill out the census forms. They are so bent on having a good time that duty to the city means nothing whatever to them.[10]

Many of the guests in a great hotel center come to the metropolis for a good time—something more thrilling and exciting than the drab monotony of Main Street. Decadence of tradition is frequently associated with the freedom and detachment that characterizes a visit in the hostelries of a great city. "Ideas of conventionality are elastic in the Grand Hotel."[11] Although a certain formal etiquette—a kind of mechanical correctness—tends to develop in the better-class hotels, the mores, that part of our tradition that is thought to involve the general welfare, weaken in this impersonal envi-

---

[9] Charles E. Merriam and Harold F. Gosnell, *Non-voting: Causes and Methods of Control* (Chicago, 1924), p. 216.
[10] Part of a front-page story in the *Seattle Daily Times* for April 12, 1930.
[11] Vicki Baum, *Grand Hotel*, p. 253.

ronment. "We are dependent for moral health upon intimate association with a group of some sort, usually consisting of family, neighbors, and other friends," wrote Professor Charles H. Cooley. "It is the interchange of ideas and feelings with this group, and a constant sense of its opinions that make ideas of right and wrong seem real to us."[12] Released from the bonds of restraint operative in smaller and more intimate circles, the individual tends to act in accordance with his impulses rather than after the pattern of the ideals and standards of his group. Among those who offend by stealing hotel property are listed "men and women who in their own communities command respect, but who, on going to a hotel, take a 'moral holiday.' "[13]

Hotel men "surely come in contact with life in all its streaked regalia," and some of them, like some newspaper men, become cynical and disillusioned. They have caught prohibitionists drunk and reformers with loose women. During the Volstead era responsible citizens and good patrons of the hotel brought in alcohol for "parties" in their rooms. Fighting and the destruction of furniture, rugs and even fixtures frequently followed.

The individual who lives continually in hotels tends to become either blasé or urbane. "I do not like to be unkind or snobbish," writes a temporary guest in a large and fashionable residential hotel, "but I have never seen such people as the majority I see here—so cheap and ostentatious in appearance—the faces a vacuum." Many become so bored with life that an auto crash on the street below does not stir them to look from the window. But on the other hand if the number and variety of stimulations to which the individual responds are not too great, he will develop an immunity to them and instead of becoming blasé or over-stimulated he

---

[12] *Social Process* (New York, 1918), p. 180.

[13] Austin G. Denniston, "Curbing the Souvenir Taker," *Hotel Management,* May, 1922, pp. 149-50.

will become urbane, poised, sophisticated, mature. Thus the individual may gradually accommodate himself to "living in public, eating in public and all but sleeping in public."

While the men living in residential hotels of the better class are usually very busy persons, the women, for the most part, find that time is their own to do with as they please. Some women in hotels are employed; a few are interested in charities and social reform; a very few have children; but many merely become mental rovers. Like the hobos described by Professor Robert E. Park, they have gained their freedom, but lost their direction.

The trouble with the hobo mind is not lack of experience, but lack of a vocation. The hobo is, to be sure, always on the move, but he has no destination, and naturally he never arrives. He has gained his freedom, but he has lost his direction.[14]

The men who patronize these same establishments are to a large extent men of affairs. They commonly regard the hotel as a convenience, a thing to be used. It is one of the great machines that serve the human race in this iron age. Such men are molded in character and personality more by the special profession or business in which they are engaged than by their place of temporary abode. Traveling about a great deal undoubtedly makes them more sophisticated, but it is only an aspect of their occupation. They have a destination, tend to make use of their experiences and are not mental rovers.

Hotel business both in Europe and America reflects fundamental fluctuations in economic and political conditions. As in other industries the decade prior to the depression was characterized by overdevelopment, and consequently the number of guests increased less rapidly than the number of rooms. The trend of business was of course markedly down-

[14] Robert E. Park, "The Mind of the Rover," *World Tomorrow*, September, 1923.

ward during the depression. If, however, the new types of wayside inns that have developed with the rise of the automobile are included, notably the cottage court and the tourist home, there has been a marked increase in the number of patrons during the past twenty years.

For more than a century foreign visitors have commented on the American habit of living permanently in hotels. The housing shortage in rapidly growing cities, the servant problem, the great mobility and restlessness of the people seem to have been factors, as well as the color and sociability of life in the small hotel or boarding house. The number who make their homes in hotels has probably increased since the World War. By 1930 the census of hotels—first of its kind in the United States—showed that in the larger cities the number of guest rooms mainly permanent was approximately equal to those mainly transient. With the decline in transient patronage during the depression the battle among hotelkeepers for the permanent guest became very severe.

The city is in general a region in which there is change and progress. Civilization grew up in cities. What the city is for life in general, the hotel is for the city. Here urbanity may be seen, as it were, through a microscope, its outstanding features enlarged and clarified. Exaggerated statements about metropolitan life—its movements, its touch-and-go neighborhoods, its vivid contrasts—become realities in the hotel environment. Problems of urban culture, such as the decline in home life, the increasing freedom and independence of women and children, the challenge of the new leisure, the disintegration of the mores—all of these are found in an accentuated form in the hotel.

PART I

HABITATS FOR TRAVELERS

CHAPTER II

CARAVANSERY TO COTTAGE COURT

THE HOTEL had its origin in the commercialization of hospitality. The free hospitality that preceded it was to a large extent a social and religious obligation. Fear of the supposed magical powers of the stranger, religious commands, need of foreign articles of trade and the desire to hear and exchange news were factors. The custom was more common in agricultural than in hunting or pastoral groups.[1] The following excerpt, for example, describes the tradition of hospitality among the maize-raising Iroquois of primeval America.

Among the Iroquois hospitality was an established usage. If a man entered an Indian house in any of their villages, whether a villager, a tribesman, or a stranger, it was the duty of the women therein to set food before him. An omission to do this would have been a discourtesy amounting to an affront. If hungry, he ate; if not hungry, courtesy required that he should taste the food and thank the giver. This would be repeated at every house he entered, and at whatever hour in the day. As a custom it was upheld by a rigorous public sentiment. The same hospitality was extended to strangers from their own and from other tribes. Upon the advent of the European race among them it was also extended to them.[2]

Among the Greeks of the Heroic Age, there was no such thing as professional innkeeping. Every stranger had the

[1] See W. E. Mühlmann, "Hospitality," *Encyclopedia of the Social Sciences*, VII, 462-63. "Hospitality is the custom of accommodating strangers in need of shelter, food and protection."

[2] From a statement by L. H. Morgan quoted in William I. Thomas, *Source Book for Social Origins* (Chicago, 1909), pp. 838-39.

right of sanctuary and asylum. Zeus Zenias, himself, watched over the security of the wayfarer. It was not until after a meal had been completed that the guest was questioned concerning his name and origin. Even today a Greek business man who recently visited his boyhood home on the island of Crete reports that a stranger in the village is asked to spend the night in a private residence.

During the fifth century B.C. the Greeks provided lodging houses in or near their temples. There were governmental inns at Delphi, home of the famous oracle. Guests were expected to leave gifts according to their means.

With the development of trade and commerce strangers came to Athens from the ends of the earth. The influx of a cosmopolitan assemblage of traders, merchants, pilgrims, art lovers, sages and Olympic games spectators created a demand for accommodations which the municipal hostelries could not meet. The professional innkeeper came into being to satisfy this demand. In Sparta, on the other hand, few inns developed. There was little commerce and only a small number of strangers. It was what would be called today "a poor hotel town."

The Roman Empire experienced a similar evolution from free to commercialized hospitality. During the period of its early history there was little need for inns. Later when Rome began to expand her power, roads were constructed, order prevailed over a wide area and travel increased. During this later period inns were fairly well provided along the great highways.

The inns and innkeepers of the ancient world seem to have been in universal disrepute. In Rome tavern-keepers were not admitted to military service and their wives or concubines were exempt from the provisions of legislation against adultery. The Roman police-soldiers classed innkeepers with thieves and gamblers. The history of inns is described by Firebaugh in his *Inns of Greece and Rome* as "an

integral part of the history of brigandage and thuggery."
There is a passage in the *Characters of Theophrastus* where he
describes an individual "so lost to shame and so lacking in
intelligence that he would even be capable of conducting a
public house." People patronizing such places took great
precautions against being seen and recognized.

St. Paul in his missionary journeys shunned the public
houses and stopped at the homes of fellow Christians. When
Greeks or Romans of the better class made a journey they
often carried their beds with them. If possible they also took
along a retinue of servants. In the warm southern climate
it was a simple matter to sleep in the open. Vehicles were
often arranged for sleeping. Many imperial officers, en route
to join outlying legions, passed nights in their carriages.

As the Roman Empire declined and the public character
degenerated, inns and taverns became increasingly popular.
Formerly patronized largely by slaves and vagabonds they
became later the haunts of the quasi-respectable. Patricians
and even emperors were frequent visitors. The tavern and
innkeeping classes came to play a major part in prolonging
the existence of pagan rites and celebrations.

These Roman hosts were the born enemies of Christian aus-
terity, they were the priests and ministers of the gods of gluttony.
They saw themselves menaced in their vital interests by a religion which enjoined abstinence and fasting upon their best
customers. Paganism with its sensual divinities, its orgies, its
sacrificial feasts, its libations in temple and tomb was the only
religion which they could embrace to their advantage and, in
defense of it, they were prepared to devote themselves, soul and
body.[3]

The barbarians that overran the Roman Empire are described as a hospitable people. The gradual spread of Chris-
tianity among them no doubt strengthened this attitude. To

[3] W. C. Firebaugh, *The Inns of Greece and Rome and a History of Hospitality
from the Dawn of Time to the Middle Ages*, p. 161.

furnish hospitality to travelers and pilgrims was one of the duties of the Christian. During medieval times abbeys and monasteries held their doors open to the wayfarer in nearly all parts of Western Europe. Rich people patronized the monasteries because they were relatively comfortable and secure. The poor visited them because there was nothing to pay. The ideal of the monk was to receive the guest as if he were Christ himself. In times of zeal this ideal might be attained. In times of laxity the rich were treated best—large contributions being expected from them—and the poor were regarded as a nuisance. Suppression of the English monasteries by Act of Parliament in 1539 encouraged the opening of more inns.

Noble guests, especially those with many servants, were apt to be too turbulent for the cloister. As a consequence the guest house was sometimes rebuilt outside the abbey gate. In this way the inn became differentiated from the less specialized monastery.

The word "inn" like the French "hotel" once meant the town residence of a nobleman. Its gradual evolution from the manor house is well described in the statement below :

Such few travelers as were benighted on the road, small merchants or pedlars going to a local fair, a knight or squire on his way to court, King's messengers and officials, would naturally put up at the manor-house. Hospitality was so rarely called for that it was willingly afforded, just as it is at an Australian homestead in the backwoods.

By the middle of the fourteenth century the roads had become more frequented, and it was no longer the fashion for the lord to reside in the comparatively humble manor-house. The cost of living had increased ; the nobility were impoverished by attendance at court, the foreign wars, and their crowd of retainers.

So the lord retired to his more secluded castle or country seat, leaving strangers to be entertained at the manor-house by a steward who afterwards was replaced by a regular innkeeper as tenant.[4]

According to Ludy in his *Historic Hotels of the World*, "historic inns or hotels exist everywhere that civilization has penetrated." The story of English inns reflects, as in other countries, the changes in manners and customs during successive periods. Many of these old inns were centers for stimulating literary discussion. Others appear in literature, such as in Shakespeare's Falstaff scenes or in Chaucer's *Canterbury Tales*. George Eliot in *Silas Marner* pictures the Rainbow Inn as a center for gossip and guzzling. The tavern was the great focus for news long before the coming of the newspaper.

An intimate relation existed in some places between the inn and the church. At 7 : 20 on Sunday evening a tourist in a little village inn remarked to the landlord, "Very quiet tonight here, isn't it?" "Well, sir," replied the innkeeper, "they bean't come out o' church yet."

Among the pleasantest memories of a pilgrimage to Walsingham, is that of a Sunday spent at a little Suffolk village, where after service Pastor and flock alike adjourned to our inn for a half an hour's gossip. The old custom would be difficult to restore nowadays, but much of the social influence of the church over the laboring classes was lost when rectors left off occupying at least once a week, the chair in the village inn parlour. For it is not without good reason that the church and inn stand so frequently side by side. Each ministers alike to the natural and common needs of man, and each in its own way has its lesson to teach us in the gospel of larger life.[5]

Old World traits of hospitality were early transplanted to America. During Spanish occupation of Florida and of the territory that is now the southwestern portion of the United

---

[4] Maskell and Gregory, *Old Country Inns of England*, pp. 5-6.
[5] *Ibid.*, p. 80.

States, travelers usually found lodgings in convents, monasteries, private homes or governors' residences. Although there are many old missions in California, no old inn dates back to the time of the padres.

In colonial Virginia it was not necessary for the traveler to pay for accommodations. His presence was a welcome break in the monotony of plantation life. This fact retarded the development of high-class hotels.

In the isolated pioneer homestead of America or Australia the stranger brought stories of adventure and news from the outside world. As a result the traveler was usually welcome and no charge was made for food and a night's lodging. Catering to the creature comforts of the stranger was simply one of the many activities that centered in the pioneer home.

The two contrasting attitudes of distrust and cordiality with which the stranger is regarded on the frontier are a familar part of my own experience. My childhood was spent on a cattle ranch in Wyoming and I recall with vividness the excitement and pleasure of having a stranger as a guest for the night or even longer, provided of course that we felt assured of his intentions and that he was good company. There were other times, however, when strangers stopped at the ranch to whom hospitality could not well be refused, for the nearest town was a day's journey away, but to whom it was grudgingly given since they were viewed with distrust as possible claim-jumpers, cattle thieves, or outlaws of one sort or another.[6]

With the decreasing isolation of American rural communities, due especially to improvements in the agencies of communication, the earlier habits of hospitality have tended to decline. In some communities certain homes began to cater to travelers ; in others, hotels developed to meet the demand.

---

[6] Margaret M. Wood, *The Stranger: a Study in Social Relationships* (New York, 1934), p. 184.

In the Pacific Northwest, where many of the pioneers are still living, grandparents tell about the time when the stranger who arrived at night was always invited to stay.

In the Old Northwest, where all the first settlers have passed, the log house was the first place of entertainment. Travelers came on horseback or by ox or horse team over primitive roads. Later, with better roads and the stage-coach, inns superseded the hospitality of the pioneers. By the time the first railroad was built many of the important highways were "beaded with taverns."

CARAVANSERY AND COACHING INN

Because hotels have arisen primarily as an accommodation to the traveler, it is obvious that their nature is fundamentally related to the kind of transportation that brings their guests. Since before the time of Christ there have existed throughout Asia stopping places along the caravan routes where men and beasts of burden were given a night's lodging. Usually there was a central space open to the skies, and around it rough sheds or roofed-in enclosures for the stabling of animals or the accommodation of travelers. The following description of the caravansery at Kuchan in the latter part of the nineteenth century is probably typical of the conditions which harassed travelers two thousand years ago. Apparently these ancient inns have changed very little through the centuries, either in architecture or in the meagerness of their conveniences.

The impossibilities of repose, and the continual irritation produced by insects brought on a kind of hectic fever which deprived me of all desire to eat. All night long three or four scores of donkeys brayed in chorus; vicious horses screamed and quarrelled, and hundreds of jackals and dogs rivalled each other in making the night hideous. After sunset the human inhabitants of the caravanserai mounted to the roof, and sat there in scanty garments, smoking their kaliouns, and talking or singing until long after midnight.[7]

The native inns of Asia change their customs more slowly than the cosmopolitan hostelries of the port cities. Provincial inns of Japan, for example, require the removal of shoes before entering, serve food on floor mats to guests seated on cushions and provide a bath for all the visitors in common without changing the water. The village inn of China is still "nothing more than a caravansery."

The wheel-barrows and carts, with their freight, are parked in the courtyard, around which are built the stables for the mules and horses. Their drivers with the barrow men sleep in the rooms adjoining the stables. Nothing but a thin partition separates them from the animals, whose munching can be heard throughout the night. The traveler carries his own bedding, which is spread out upon a few boards stretched over two trestles. The accommodations are rude, but the food is wholesome and abundant, and when one has ridden twenty or thirty miles sleep, even on a board, is sound and healthful.[8]

"Coaching inns" developed to meet the needs of stagecoach travelers in Western Europe and in the American colonies. Among these needs the wish for security was at first dominant.

---

[7] Quoted in W. C. Firebaugh, *op. cit.*, pp. 24-26.

[8] Edward T. Williams, *China: Yesterday and Today* (New York, 1923), p. 125. "On all the principal lines of road throughout India, the Government has erected bungalows, at intervals of from ten to twenty miles, for the accommodation of European travellers. The natives have their *serais*, resembling the Turkish khans, and unless travelling by post, are not admitted into the bungalows. The latter are plain but substantial cottages, furnished only with tables, chairs, and bedsteads, and generally containing two dining and two sleeping apartments. There are outhouses for the residence of a servant, called a *peon*, who has charge of the establishment, and for the cooks, or messmen, who are obliged to procure supplies and prepare meals according to a fixed scale of prices." [Bayard Taylor, *A Visit to India, China and Japan in the Year 1853* (New York, 1869), pp. 67-68.]

The coaches started on their journey each morning and evening from great inn yards surrounded by tiers of galleries one above the other. Sometimes, as at the *Bull and Mouth* in St. Martins le Grand, or the *Oxford Arms* in Warwick Lane, there were four stories of these galleries. It is not easy to trace the various steps by which the plan of the coaching inn was evolved from the "corrall" of migrating tribes, who when resting for the night arranged their wagons in a hollow square, with their cattle in the center. But the idea underlying the coaching inn was a species of fortress entered only by the great archway with massive doors strongly barred at closing time. The bed-chambers of the guests all opened into galleries overlooking the yard. When an alarm was raised each owner of wagons or cattle in the yard could at once hurry out to the defense of his property.[9]

Travelers during the seventeenth and eighteenth centuries stress the crudities and hardships of the inns. With certain exceptions they seem to agree in condemning the beds, food and other accommodations in the inns of France, Italy and Germany. By the second half of the eighteenth century, however, coach traffic in England could be relied upon. There were also regular stage-wagons both to and from London and on the crossroads. It is probably significant, however, that even during this period the gentry preferred to travel in their own carriages.

The bicycle and more recently the motor car have revived interest in these roads and inns of the past. The motorist in England is greeted by such interesting signs as The Three Horse Shoes, Coach and Horses, George in the Tree, the Porridge Pot, the Rose and Crown, the Plough, Fox and Hounds, the Haystack, the Golden Lion and the Saracen's Head. In France, Italy, Austria and Germany, relics of coaching days can also be seen. Closer inspection of these establishments reveals interesting changes, however. The en-

---

[9] Maskell and Gregory, *op. cit.*, pp. 82-83.

trance for the coach and a large courtyard may still be retained, but the stables have usually been converted into garages. In general the prices are not designed for the economical traveler.

You have probably heard and read so many delightful things about the "old English inns" that your first thought will be to look for one of these. There are dozens of them in Stratford, charming-looking old places, with hewn beams and quaintly-sagging roofs. But don't be tempted. For once inside, instead of the shining kitchen that Washington Irving so eloquently described, there will be a dapper little gentleman who will ask you if you care for a room with private bath, and will inform you coolly that a bed and breakfast will cost you twelve shillings.[10]

As in England, the establishment of post roads in the colonies improved and multiplied the inns. Travel increased. There was really only one main artery of traffic, however, that from Boston through New York and Philadelphia to Baltimore. Early European travelers who wrote books about their American experiences followed this route.

Many old inns have been linked with drunkenness and debauchery. Many have also been important social centers. The landlord of colonial times may not have been the greatest man in town, but he was usually the best known. The extent to which the tavern served as a social center may be seen in the following selection :

The tavern was the most important place in town ; it was the gathering place to learn the news, it was the business exchange for the neighborhood, the place where bargains were made and prices learned and quoted. It was at once the town hall and assembly room, the courthouse and the show-room, the hotel and the exchange. Itinerant actors and showmen gave their exhibitions in its public room, strange animals and curiosities were displayed at the tavern, here were the bulletin boards contain-

---

[10] Frank Schoonmaker, *Through Europe on Two Dollars a Day* (New York, 1927), p. 184.

ing the lists of jurors, the notices of vendues, legal notices, rewards for runaway slaves or servants, for lost animals or other property, and the farmer's advertisements of what he had to sell or what he wanted to buy.[11]

The importance of the tavern to the village in which it was located seems to have been greater than its importance to travelers. This rôle as social center for the colonial community, in addition to its tendency to divide the village into two conflicting groups, has been well described by Small and Vincent.

The tavern or hotel holds an important place in the community as the temporary home of many of the men who are either unmarried or have left their families behind, and as the halting-place of the stage-coach, which connects the village with the outside world. It is, therefore, a rendezvous for some of the most active elements of the population. There is, besides, a barroom which provides a convenient and comfortable place for social intercourse, and furnishes means of conviviality. Many things combine to make the tavern attractive to a large class in the community, and yet the sale of liquor, the card-playing, often for high stakes, and the questionable character of many who frequent the place, repel an even greater number of citizens. The establishment, however, seems to meet, as no other institution does, certain demands for a place of resort for casual conversation, for discussion of local interests, and for planning public measures. Yet it is a source of separation in the community. Many men refuse to go there, while, on the other hand, its supporters are disinclined to meet at the store or elsewhere.[12]

FROM INN TO HOTEL

The French word "hotel" did not come into general use prior to the nineteenth century. Its use marks the develop-

[11] Stephen Jenkins, *The Old Boston Post Road*, p. 32. Americans used the word "tavern" in place of the English term "inn."

[12] Quoted in Newell L. Sims, *The Rural Community* (New York, 1920), pp. 342-43.

ment of something more luxurious in the housing of guests. The "bowl and pitcher" period in the evolution of American hotels is said to have begun with the opening of the Tremont House in Boston in 1829. Few inns had exceeded thirty rooms in size, yet the Tremont had a grand total of one hundred and seventy—"the world's largest" at that time. Although it had been customary in colonial times for the traveler to share his bedroom or even his bed with one or more strangers, the Tremont introduced the unique feature of specializing in single and double rooms for its guests. Sometimes when visitors did not behave, the innkeeper, who was held responsible for the character of his guests, put them in the stocks; but Mine Host at the Tremont started a new policy of giving the traveler the utmost in comfort, luxury and service. This service included such novelties as an individual lock on the door, a bowl and pitcher and free soap for every guest room.

With the industrial revolution in occidental nations came the development of the railroad and the steamship.

> We hear no more of the clanging hoof
> And the stage coach rattling by;
> For the steam king rules the troubled world,
> And the old Pike's left to die.[13]

It was this shift to steam transportation, together with the moneyed middle classes produced by the industrial revolution, that facilitated the development of the hotel in the modern sense of that word. Just as many innkeepers had operated stage lines, so "hotel men built, or helped to build, many railroads and many railroad companies built hotels."

Not only did the word hotel come to be more frequently applied to the larger hostelries in England in the early years of the nineteenth century, but the period saw the primitive inn transformed into a more complete type of shelter for the traveler.

---

[13] Jenkins, *op. cit.*, p. 42.

When the stage coach lines were at the zenith of their importance in England, the coaching houses or inns represented the
best accommodation a traveler in that country could expect. At
the termini of the coach lines and at important posting houses
along the roads, where horses were changed, were to be found
the coaching inns. This system has been transferred to the railroads which followed the stage coaches, and all of the railroads
of England have hotels attached to their important stations, a
method which is found in only a very few instances in the United
States.

The last quarter of the nineteenth century witnessed decided
improvement in the design, capacity and speed of trans-Atlantic
steamships, and in the great number of voyagers from the United
States to the Old World. British hotels not only increased in
number but were provided with many attractions which were
not lost on the tourists.[14]

In this evolution from inn to hotel profound changes have
taken place. The relation between Mine Host and his guest
in the inns and taverns of the past was personal and hospitable. If the proprietor of a large modern hostelry ever sees
his patrons it is probably at some big public dinner. The
present-day hotel is a great institution whose keynote is impersonality. Charles Dickens was probably the first writer
to see the fundamental significance of these changes.

We all know the great station hotel belonging to the company
of proprietors, which has suddenly sprung up in the back out-
skirts of any place we like to name, and where we look out of
our palatial windows, at little back yards and gardens, old summer houses, fowl-houses, pigeon-traps, and pigsties. We all know
this hotel in which we can get anything we want, after its kind,
for money ; but where nobody is glad to see us, or sorry to see
us, or minds (our bill paid) whether we come or go, or how, or
when, or cares about us. We all know this hotel where we have
no individuality, but put ourselves into the general post, as it

---

[14] Adapted from Robert B. Ludy, *Historic Hotels of the World*, pp. 159-60.
Quoted by permission of the David McKay Company, publishers.

were, and are sorted and disposed of according to our division. We all know that we can get on very well indeed at such a place, but still not perfectly well; and this may be because the place is largely wholesale, and there is a lingering personal retail interest within us that asks to be satisfied.[15]

Various "newfangled notions" have made the rivalry between American hotels "a sort of game, like the annual blooming of new models of motor cars and radio sets." It was these devices, according to Jefferson Williamson in *The American Hotel*, that "made the modern hotels modern." The most important among them are (1) modern plumbing, especially the hotel bathroom; (2) the installation of heating systems; (3) the "vertical railway" or elevator; (4) the electric light and (5) the telephone.

The history of hotel-keeping in such cities as Chicago, San Francisco and New Orleans has followed much the same general outline:

—first the crude, makeshift taverns of early pioneer days, run by a landlord and his family; then the small hotels with something of the luxuries and comforts of the hotels of the East; and finally, a grand hotel of the New York palace pattern, often the largest and most expensive building in town.[16]

The Evolution of the Auto Camp

Just as the inn developed in response to travel in animal-drawn vehicles and the hotel in response to the growth of railroads and the steamship, so the automobile tourist camp

---

[15] Quoted in Thomas Burke, *The Book of the Inn* (New York, 1927), pp. 58-59. Oscar Tschirky, *maitre d'hotel* at the Waldorf-Astoria, "has acted as official host during the past forty years to more celebrated persons and world leaders than probably any other living man has ever met. . . . In these days when the average hotel is a vast, smoothly-run machine, Oscar remains the modern personification of the traditional Mine Host of the old-time inn." [Henry B. Lent, *The Waldorf-Astoria* (New York, 1934), pp. 39-40].

[16] Adapted from Jefferson Williamson, *The American Hotel: An Anecdotal History*, p. 77.

has developed as a new type of habitat for the traveler in response to the development of the automobile and automobile touring. Its housekeeping facilities have enabled many people to tour who would not otherwise be able to travel. Although accurate facts about the evolution of this new variety of roadside inn are not available for the country as a whole, studies on the Pacific Coast indicate that the trend during the past decade has been from the municipal tenting camp to the private cottage court.[17] Few cabins were available for tourists until 1924 and these were mostly shacks. In 1929, however, a study of 714 auto camps in Western Oregon and Washington and in southwestern British Columbia showed that 551, or 77 per cent, were cabin camps with a total of 5,450 cottages. As in the case of older types of transient habitats an increasing differentiation in the prices, physical equipment, and patronage of auto camps has taken place in response to demands from both laboring and business classes.

The passing of the municipal tourist camp seems to have been due to the opposition of both the hotel men and the owners of private camps. A leading Canadian Boniface wrote as follows:

Tourist camps to me are a bugbear, and one of the chief menaces to profitable hotel operation in this country. They are generally supported by Government or Municipal funds which places them in the position of unfair competition.

Mr. Clinton A. Ambrose, secretary of the Oregon Auto Camp Association, made the following statement in his annual report for 1928:

This association continues its protest against subsidized city operated tourist camps. These camps are maintained in compe-

---

[17] See Norman S. Hayner, "The Auto Camp as a New Type of Hotel," *Sociology and Social Research*, March-April, 1931, pp. 365-72 and "Auto Camps in the Evergreen Playground," *Social Forces*, December, 1930, pp. 256-66.

tition with private enterprise which is taxed directly or indi-
rectly for their maintenance.

Maps showing the geographical distribution of auto camps
in the Pacific Northwest suggest a rough classification into
two types : (1) commercial or en route camps located on or
near the main highways and (2) resort or terminal camps
located in the mountains or on the water at objective points
for vacationing. There are also camps that combine the
characteristics of the en route and terminal types. A large
"tourist colony" half-way between Jacksonville and Miami,
Florida, for example, houses many overnight guests. There
is also a group of small business men, mechanics and ex-
farmers from the Middle West who have saved enough to
spend the winter months here. A study of Southern California auto courts suggests an economic classification into
two fundamental types : (1) the older auto camps with a predominantly working-class patronage and (2) well-equipped
cottage courts catering to the business classes.

The advantages which the better type of private cottage
court presents in competition with the hotel for motor tourist patronage may perhaps best be presented in the language
of an auto camp owner :

When the traveler drives under the shed of his cabin he is at
home and can feel at ease. Stopping at hotels he has to take out
what baggage he needs and have it lugged to his room while he
takes his car to some garage and walks back. He has been traveling all day, his clothes are wrinkled and dusty, and he feels
grimy. When he registers he thinks everyone is looking him over.
When he cleans up for dinner, he finds the clothing that was
packed in the car all mussed up. If he changes he is conscious of
his appearance, even though no one is paying any attention to
him. There is no place to sit around where he can get fresh air.
In the morning he has to get his car from the garage and pack
his baggage in front of the hotel. When he settles up he is out

about three times as much as if he had stopped in a good camp and has felt like a bum all the time.

On the other hand, the advantages which the first-class hotel offers the tourist are suggested by the following excerpt from a letter written by the manager of a leading hostelry :

I realize what keen competition the auto camp gives to the second and third-rate hotels. The fact that people are close to their cars and baggage and can get their own meals for very reasonable prices has been the main thing that has induced them to use the tourist camps. It is practically impossible for the smaller hotels to furnish anything to offset this combination. One of the things that is our salvation in a hotel of this class, however, is that the average person enjoys comfort and likes to follow the line of least resistance. It is far easier for the tourist party having plenty of money to let the bellboys and porters handle the baggage and the doorman take the car to the garage where it will be washed up and well cared for. The women in the party do not have to set a house to rights or cook meals.

Historical consideration of habitats for travelers suggests three major types (1) the inn, (2) the hotel, and (3) the cottage court. The inn, of which the caravansery was merely a crude variety, developed in response to animal-drawn transportation. Its name suggests the open inner court, or patio, for camels, donkeys or stage-coaches. The hotel is a larger and more comfortable institution. Its rise was associated with the coming of the railroad and the steamship. The resort hotel caters to people who wish to get close to the heart of nature in a luxurious way.[18] Wherever the western machine civilization has penetrated hotels have tended to replace the native inns. The cottage court is a recent transient habitat peculiar to America. Europe does not have it. Its separate cottage units and its motor tourist patronage differentiate it from other types.

---

[18] The resort hotel is discussed in chap. X.

CHAPTER III

HOTELS AND URBAN AREAS

THE AREA in which a hotel is located plays an important part in determining its character. Like any other institution, to be understood it must be seen in its social and economic setting. All large American cities tend to have neighborhoods with similar characteristics. The more mobile of these local communities are marked by their own distinctive habitats for travelers. The area of greatest mobility, the central business district, has its commercial hotel. In the zone of deterioration outside the city center, the hobo area has its lodging house and "the world of furnished rooms" its rooming house. Residential hotels are usually found in the more accessible parts of the residential zone.

Hotel life is, of course, a transient life. Tradition does not identify the inn with permanent residence. The percentage of transient guests varies, however, in different types of hotels. Transient hotels sell their rooms on a daily basis. The average stay is usually less than a week. Residential hotels, on the other hand, sell their rooms for longer periods and their leases are at lower than day by day rates. In this shifting population a guest who remains a month or more is generally considered a "permanent." Consequently the relative number of transient and permanent guests in a hotel help to classify it. "A hotel is classed as 'transient' if more than 75 per cent of its patrons are transient; as 'permanent' if more than 75 per cent of its patrons are permanent; and as 'mixed' if not as much as 75 per cent of its patronage is one way or the other."[1] Of the more than 13,000

---

[1] *Census of Hotels*, 1930, p. 3.

hotels included in the United States Census three-eighths were listed as mainly transient; one-eighth as mainly permanent; and one-half as mixed transient and permanent.

Studies of Chicago and of the leading cities of the Pacific Coast indicate that the percentage of transiency in hotels tends to decrease as the distance in time and cost from the city center increases. The leading transient hotels of the American city are likely to be located in the central business district on sites readily accessible to the shopping and theatre areas and to the means of transportation. Residential hotels usually occupy the more attractive sites outside of and yet accessible to the business center. But from the standpoint of the area in which the hotel is located—whether a business district, a slum or a residential neighborhood—its population is always relatively transient.

Located in the transition zone between the business district and the residential areas is the lodging house, a marginal type of hotel. Because of the seasonal and cyclical fluctuations of present-day industrial society it has become more and more necessary for wage earners to travel from place to place. For these footloose, homeless men the lodging house or "stag hotel" is a low-priced, temporary domicile. Nels Anderson, author of *The Hobo*, differentiates clearly between the lodging house and the legitimate hotel.

A lodging house may be a dormitory, but more often the beds are separated by dwarfed partitions which do not reach the ceiling, thus forming tiny rooms known in the United States and in England as cubicles and in France as *chambrettes*. Other characteristics of the lodging house are the segregation of the sexes and the preponderance of men. . . . A further feature which distinguishes the lodging house from the hotel and which has grown out of its function as a cheap and temporary form of accommodation is its right to refuse shelter to undesirable applicants.

A flop house is a lodging house of the dormitory type but with much lower prices than other lodging places. The better grade of flop house provides bed and bedding; there is a lower grade which provides only the bare bunks or chairs, and the lowest permits men for a pittance to sleep on the floor.[2]

The "service" in one of the better New York lodging houses of 1899 was the tramp's "nearest approach to hotel life" according to Josiah Flynt.

At twenty and twenty-five cents a night a man can have a little room to himself; by "room" I mean a sort of cell without a roof, in which is a cot, a chair (sometimes) and a locker. I slept in one of these houses in the Bowery one night. The office and sitting room were comparatively cozy, and they were respectable so far as dress and general manners were concerned. Upstairs in the sleeping-apartment things were not so pleasant. There was a bad odor about everything, and the beds were decidedly unclean, as are most beds in most lodging-houses. I left word at the office that I wished to be called at seven o'clock in the morning, and my order was distinctly obeyed. At about half-past six I was awakened by a man poking me in the ribs with a long stick leveled at me over the partition-wall. After the man had poked me with the stick, he said, "Eh, bloke, time to get up."[3]

Depending on the point of view, Y. M. C. A. and Y. W. C. A. hotels are either high-class lodging houses or third-rate hotels. Although their guests are usually housed in rooms rather than in cubicles, they do retain the right to refuse shelter to undesirable visitors. The high percentage of church members among their patrons and the low proportion who use tobacco reveal the selective influence of a religious management.

Although the term "lodging house" is also applied to the rooming house in England and in parts of the United States,

---

[2] Adapted from *Encyclopedia of the Social Sciences*, IX, 595-97. Used by permission of the Macmillan Company, publishers.

[3] *Tramping With Tramps* (New York, 1899), p. 123.

notably Boston, a clear distinction should be made between these two transient habitats.

The distinction between the cheap, transient lodging-house and the rooming-house lies in the class of patrons, in prices charged, and in method of payment. The lodgers in a rooming-house pay by the week or month, those in a cheap lodging-house by the night. The "roomers" pay from one to seven dollars a week and are both men and women; the patron of the cheap lodging-house pays from five to twenty-five cents a night, and is generally a man, although there are in the larger cities cheap lodging-houses for women also.[4]

"On the edge of the slums there are likely to be regions, already in process of being submerged, characterized as the 'rooming-house areas,' the dwelling places of bohemians, transient adventurers of all sorts, and the unsettled young folk of both sexes."[5] The "world of furnished rooms" of Chicago's Near North Side has been described by Harvey W. Zorbaugh as "a world of atomized individuals, of spiritual nomads." In contrast to the homeless men of the lodging houses these roomers are typically "white collar" office workers.

The constant comings and goings of its inhabitants is the most striking and significant characteristic of this world of furnished rooms. This whole population turns over every four months. There are always cards in the windows, advertising the fact that rooms are vacant, but these cards rarely have to stay up over a day, as people are constantly walking the streets looking for rooms. The keepers of the rooming-houses change almost as rapidly as the roomers themselves. At least half of the keepers of these houses have been at their present addresses six months or less.[6]

---

[4] A. B. Wolfe, *The Lodging House Problem in Boston*, pp. 1-2.

[5] Robert E. Park, "The Concept of Position in Sociology," *Publications of the American Sociological Society*, XX (1925), 8.

[6] Harvey W. Zorbaugh, *The Gold Coast and the Slum*, pp. 71-72.

Different hotel areas tend to be more or less clearly defined in any large city. The de luxe hotels of London, for example, are located in the West End from Hyde Park east to the Thames. To the northeast of this area in Bloomsbury and to the southwest in Earl's Court and South Kensington are cheaper residential hostelries. In the drab working-class East End there are no hotels. In Berlin there is the older central section, the "Centrum," with its tourist hotels, its museums and palaces and its broad boulevard, Unter den Linden. West of the large Tiergarten is the newer and more fashionable district, known locally as the "Zoo," with its leading movie palaces and restaurants, its Kurfürsten Damn Avenue and its first-class hostelries. Paris has its Left Bank and Right Bank of the Seine. On the more plebian and colorful Left is the Latin Quarter with many cheap hotels, some of them patronized by university students. On the Right are the forty first-class hotels. There also is a distinct movement of business westward toward the now fashionable Etoile neighborhood. As in other European cities many second-class hotels of Paris are located near the railroad stations. Here the guest does not need to hire a taxi, but can carry his own baggage.

The Mid-town hotel area of New York includes huge transient caravanseries like the Statler, New Yorker and Pennsylvania—much larger houses of hospitality than any to be found in European cities. Some distance to the south on Manhattan Island is the Bowery lodging house district where the hobo has his nearest approach to hotel life. Since the hotel patrons in the Broadway theatre area to the north are for the most part "sporting" people, the house counts are high on Saturday night. On the East Side along Park Avenue, where the new Waldorf-Astoria is located, and near Central Park still farther to the north, is the real wealth and "society." On the West Side along Riverside Drive is the would-be "society," the *nouveau riche*.

As in other American cities most of Chicago's leading hotels are located in its central business district. Here is the Stevens, which, with three thousand rooms, is the largest hotel dream that has yet materialized. All of the first-class hotels in the Windy City are situated either on or within a few blocks of the Lake Michigan shore. In fact hotels tend to form a line from Evanston on the north to Woodlawn on the south. Outside the Loop the most important clusters are in the Wilson Avenue District on the fashionable "Gold Coast" and in Hyde Park on the South Side. Hyde Park and the North Shore form the "Promised Land" of the Jewish community.

The latest avenue of escape from the ghetto is represented by the rapid influx of Jews into the apartment and residential hotels of Chicago, particularly of Hyde Park and the North Shore. So popular have these hotels become with the Jewish population that a "Jewish Hotel Row" is rapidly springing up. The middle-class business men among the Jews moved into these hotels originally, not merely because their wives wanted to be free from household duties, nor merely because they had reached a station in life where they could afford the luxuries of hotel life, but rather because they wished to be taken for successful business or professional men—not merely successful Jews. The hotels offered anonymity; they offered freedom from ritual and the close supervision of the intimate community. Here one could be one's self, and, if one spent a little occasionally on parties, dinners, and entertainment, and if one "Americanized" one's name and put up a good front by playing golf and being a good sport, one could get to know the best people and break into gentile society.[7]

The racial and immigrant groups that concentrate in our great cities tend to develop their own houses of hospitality. There are of course many more Jewish than Negro hotels. The transient nature of hotel life seems to attract a type of individual fitted by temperament and experience to a mo-

---

[7] Adapted from Louis Wirth, *The Ghetto* (Chicago, 1928), pp. 257-58.

bile existence. "Reared in intimate association with the bustle and business of the market place, constantly intent on the fascinating game of buying and selling, 'the Wandering Jew' has neither opportunity nor inclination to cultivate that intimate attachment to places and persons which is characteristic of the immobile person."[8]

Nevertheless, although less mobile than the Jew, the Negro is also traveling and living in hotels. In fact the big difference between freedom and slavery is precisely this liberty to move. The Negro tenant forced consideration from the planter by his right to move from one plantation to another. At first there were no Negro hotels and, since Negroes were not admitted to white hostelries, the traveling members of the race stopped at private homes. Undoubtedly some of the most favored homes eventually developed into hotels. In any case at the present time Negro hotels are to be found in every large American city.

In the bigger cities there tend to be distinct gradations among the various Negro hotels. The Vincennes Hotel in Chicago, for example, has been called "The Drake of the Black Belt." "There are other places," said the enterprising mulatto owner and manager, "but look at them—only rooming houses." Most of the guests are business and professional people—physicians, lawyers and a few manufacturers—with a sprinkling of highly-paid workmen, such as plasterers. Negro conventions make their headquarters at the Vincennes. Dusky debutantes, the social élite of the "Black Belt," "come out" here.

Although only eleventh in population San Francisco ranks next to New York and Chicago in the total number of full-time guest rooms reported by the 1930 Hotel Census. The fact that Los Angeles is fourth, Seattle sixth, and Portland eighth, in this same series, suggests a greater mobility of population on the Pacific Coast than in other sections of the

---

[8] Thomas, *op. cit.*, p. 169.

country. Recency of settlement, seaboard location of cities, the high percentage of native-born in the population, and the active advertising of scenic and climatic attractions are no doubt factors increasing the travel habit. There is also a seasonal flow of tourists and workers up and down the Coast. While the summer heat of the sunny southland encourages a northward movement of California's pleasure seekers and migratory laborers, the rainy winter months in the evergreen forest belt of the north stimulate a reciprocal flow of people from Oregon, Washington and Western Canada.

In proportion to its population more full-time hotel guest rooms were reported by the 1930 Hotel Census for Seattle than for any other city in the United States having a population of 250,000 and over. Seattle had 72 hotel rooms per thousand population. San Francisco came second with 62.

As suggested above, summer is the tourist season in Seattle. This period is also popular for conventions. These visitors increase the house count and percentage of transiency in the better-class hotels. In winter the same hotels may have as many guests, but the percentage of permanents is higher. Cheap hotels exhibit the reverse in seasonal fluctuations. With the exception of a short period of lively business before and after the Fourth of July, winter is the big season. During that period the migratory worker returns to the "skid-road" area of the metropolis. A study of the daily house counts in a typical working-man's hotel over the period of a pre-depression year indicates that December and January are the peak months, with the hotel filled to capacity during Christmas week. During the remainder of the year this hotel averages a house count of only three-fifths its capacity.

According to a student survey of Seattle hotels made during the pre-depression year of 1927, in the representative month of November, 437 places, listed as hotels in the state hotel inspector's files,[9] were found by investigation to be in operation and to contain a total of 27,012 guest rooms. Almost one-third of these hotels were operated by Japanese and 125 of them, with an aggregate of 8,957 rooms, were members of the Japanese Hotel Association. In sixty-eight of the associated Japanese hotels all the guests were white; in fifty-one they were of various races, with whites predominating in thirty-one, Japanese in eleven, Filipinos in six, Chinese in two, and Negroes in one; in two the guests were all Negroes; in only four were they all Japanese. Japanese hotels cater for the most part to workingmen who prefer them because they are newer, cleaner, cheaper, and quieter than most American lodging houses. Some of the Seattle hotels, however, cater to middle-class Americans. An American woman who is living in one of them reports the following experience:

When I first came to this hotel the proprietor was American. While I was still living here he sold out to a Japanese family and as I felt that I did not wish to live in a Japanese hotel, I planned to move. My friends thought that the place had lost its respectability and urged me to leave. It was inconvenient for me to go immediately so I decided to stay a few days though I felt inferior for doing it, as if I were living in the slums. After two days, however, I was ashamed of my attitude, and let my friends know of my intention to stay. The Japanese manager was all that could be desired. Everything was clean and quiet and two or three times every day the proprietor's young daughter would shyly knock at my door to see if I wished anything. The service was so thoroughly satisfactory that now I see no reason for going to a less commodious place simply because the manager is an American.

---

[9] The hotel is defined legally in the State of Washington as any building or dwelling which contains five bedrooms to be rented out to transient guests either by the day or the week. Although this includes a number of borderline types, it stresses mobility of population which is fundamental. The fee charged for the annual inspection is based on the number of bedrooms.

First-class hotels must retain a reputation for respectability or travelers will not patronize them and their value will depreciate. These so-called "decent hotels" should be clearly distinguished from houses of ill-repute. The cheap hotels, usually located in the transition zone that tends to form around the central business district of every American city, do not try so hard to maintain a good reputation. In fact, as neighborhoods deteriorate with the expansion of the city, once respectable hotels may eventually become notorious as resorts for disorderly conduct. Two investigators in Seattle reported the following experience with a house of ill-repute :

It was after midnight when we walked up to the .... hotel in Chinatown. This is a small two-story building that is not large enough to accommodate many guests. There was a pair of swinging doors halfway up the wide steps and an office at the head of the stairs. As we were standing in the office, a young, good-looking girl, scantily clad, came out of the room on the left.

"Did you boys want something?"

"Yes," I said, "we'd like to get a room for the night."

"Just a minute, I'll get someone."

While she was gone we looked at the register. About half of the residences listed were Bremerton (a satellite, navy-yard city). I afterwards learned that this hotel had the reputation for having the prettiest prostitutes in Seattle and that most of the girls were in their early twenties. Its reputation had at least reached Bremerton. The sailors did not appear to be backward about signing their true names.

An older woman appeared and gave us the price of the rooms. We decided they were too high and left.

HOTEL HINTERLANDS

Hotels are not only situated in a local community; they also have a position in the larger economic region. In general the leading metropolitan hostelries draw from a wider area than less important hotels. The nine most important cities

4

from which the Olympic in Seattle draws its patronage are all, with the exception of Seattle itself, outside of the Puget Sound region. On the basis of September and December registrations for 1930 New York and Chicago ranked fifth and seventh respectively. The other seven cities were all on the Pacific Coast with San Francisco, Portland and Los Angeles leading. Smaller second or third-rate hotels show a much larger proportion of their registrations from the Seattle metropolitan region.

The metropolitan region is primarily a functional entity. Geographically it extends as far as the city exerts a dominant influence. The basic elements of its structural pattern are centers, routes, and rims. It represents a constellation of centers, the interrelations of which are characterized by dominance and subordination. Every region is organized around a central city or focal point of dominance in which are located the institutions and services that cater to the region as a whole and integrate it with other regions.[10]

The term *hinterland* may be used to describe the area from which a hotel's guests most frequently come. Just as there is a close functional relation between the metropolis and its hinterland, so also does a particular hotel enterprise reflect the area which it serves.

The automobile seems to have had a discouraging effect on the hotel business in the small settlements of the metropolitan region. Hotel inspection data in the State of Washington show that during the decade 1921 to 1930 the number of hotel rooms has decreased in the smaller centers, especially those having a population less than 1,000, and increased in larger places. A letter of inquiry to Mr. L. M. Rickerd, under whose direction hotels were inspected, brought the following explanation:

During the past ten years there has been quite a change in hotel conditions due largely to the development of transporta-

---

[10] Adapted from R. D. McKenzie, *The Metropolitan Community*, p. 70.

tion. A person traveling from a central point can go a distance of many miles, take care of his business and return home the same day. Many of the outlying districts where the hotel business was very good in 1920, have closed several hotels and you will find only one doing a very small business.

Hotels and camps located on the rim of the metropolitan region commonly experience two types of weekly fluctuation. Resorts have their best business on the week-ends; commercial houses show a high count during the middle of the week. Every favorable week-end there is an outflow of people from the various Pacific Coast cities to enjoy the wide variety of recreational facilities advertised by the surrounding girdle of mountain and beach resorts. A counter movement is made by traveling salesmen who arrange their schedules so they may spend Saturday night amid the bright lights of the larger center.

The length of time a transient guest will stay in a given place seems to vary directly with the size of the city. John Willy, editor of *The Hotel Monthly*, came to this conclusion as long ago as 1907.

A large proportion of the rooms in New York hotels are arranged in parlor, bedroom, and bathroom suites. The reason is that many visitors in New York make a prolonged stay—one, two, three weeks, a month, or longer—and the parlor or sitting room is a necessity, especially when the visitors have callers. In other cities the call for suites of this kind is less than half what it is in New York and in St. Louis it is less than it is in Chicago, the average stay being under two days. In small country towns the average is less than a day of twenty-four hours.[11]

In 1933 the average stay of guests in the better-class hotels of New York City was 3.6 days; in Chicago, 3.1; in Philadelphia, 2.9; in Detroit and Cleveland, 2.2; and in Columbus, 2.1. The average stay of guests in these six cities, all of

[11] Adapted from "Seeing New York," *The Hotel Monthly*, February, 1907

which are over 250,000 in population, was 2.7. In five cities under 250,000 the average was 1.6.[12]

Guests whose homes are nearer to the large city tend to stay a shorter period of time than those living at a greater distance. The management of one of the large hotels in New York City, for example, grouped its registrations for the year 1926 from the various states of the country into geographical zones. For practical purposes they thought of the states composing any zone as homogeneous in character. The states in the northeastern section of the country were grouped into three zones according to the volume of business in relation to their population. Zone I comprising eight states nearest to New York had 490 annual registrations in the hotel per 100,000 of the population. Zone II, roughly semi-circular in shape, had 182 registrations and Zone III, which was for the most part farther away, had 82. In Zone IV were placed the southern states with a rate of 77; in Zone V, all of the western states with 73. The average lengths of stay for guests coming from the successive zones were: I, 2.2 days; II, 3.1; III, 3.3; IV, 5.0; V, 6.3. The same general principle was supported by studies of the registrations in similar hotels located in Cleveland and St. Louis.

Hotel hinterlands change with economic and political fluctuations. Because of the many crowded nations struggling against each other with varying success Europe illustrates this point more dramatically than North America. Radical changes took place in the tourist movements of Europe during the Great War and the Great Depression. Tourist traffic to Vienna from the Austro-Hungarian Empire, to cite an example, increased steadily from 1874, when the earliest statistics are available, up to the time of the war. The movement from countries constituting the former empire declined about half during the war, but had increased by 1930 to a

---

[12] Data from E. M. Bywell, office manager, Horwath and Horwath, hotel accountants.

point almost as high as that in 1910. Although in 1913 the tourist traffic from outside the empire was only one-fourth that from within, after the war, encouraged by the Austrian inflation, it increased rapidly to a point approaching five-sixths.[13] The number of American travelers staying at Viennese hotels in 1927 was more than twice as large as the number in 1912.[14] With the coming of the depression, however, the tourist traffic to Vienna from foreign countries fell off markedly.

In the following interview the Herr Direktor von Wien,[15] one of the leading hotel men in this cosmopolitan city, contrasts vividly the Hapsburg and Socialist Viennas. He makes the interesting distinction between travel that is organic and travel that is artificially stimulated. The sources of travel under these contrasting situations compose two fundamentally different hinterlands.

Before the war Austria-Hungary was an empire with fifty-one million people.[16] English aristocrats used to come to Austria for grouse hunting. Austrian aristocrats were in turn entertained in England with fox hunts. There was the excitement of racing in the fall and spring; of theatres and court balls in the winter. Officers in the army of 300,000 men were urged by their wives or by their growing daughters to come to Vienna. Vienna was the intellectual center of the Near East. There was no need for a Tourist Bureau. Travel was organic, i.e., it came from various parts of the empire without artificial stimulation.

Important socially were the movements of the imperial court. Bad Ischl, the site of the emperor's summer palace, was the center of fashion for the warmer season.

---

[13] Based on data compiled by Diplomkaufmann H. A. R. Ortner in an unpublished manuscript on "Der Wiener Fremdenverkehr 1874-1931" at the University of Vienna.

[14] *Statistique Internationale des Grandes Villes*, p. 286.

[15] In this and in similar documents presented later, names of managers and of hotels are fictitious.

[16] Austria now has only six and one-half millions.

Since their wives at home had become only housekeepers, men from Poland liked to come to Vienna for a good time. Here they could mix in "society" and meet other women.

If they could afford it, difficult cases from as far as Turkey came to Vienna for medical work. I can remember seeing as a boy the carriages that brought Turkish families through the archway that is now filled by my office. I can remember their servants and their primitive habits. The hospital was built by the Emperor Joseph in the latter part of the eighteenth century. It was a mecca for Southeastern Europe. From an area extending as far as Persia students came to Vienna to study medicine and law. There was a large percentage of foreigners in the high schools.

Before the war the natural movement of travel was eastward from Paris through Munich and Vienna to Constantinople. During the war connections between France, Italy, Yugo-Slavia and Roumania were improved. Now traffic is routed that way. Going east from Paris the traveler, especially if he stops en route, must go through German, Czecho-Slovakian, Austrian, Hungarian and Yugo-Slav customs and monetary restrictions. It is a much more difficult task to route a traveler through these countries— get visas, inform him about exchange rates and money regulations—than in an Ask-Mr.-Foster office in the United States. An eminent French expert on tourist traffic insists that this route must again be made more facile for tourists.

Russians used to come in large numbers through Austria and Southern Germany on their way to the Riviera. With the revolution of 1917 this movement was cut off.[17] Students from Roumania, Bulgaria and Yugo-Slavia flow toward Paris now. Paris has, in fact, become the intellectual center for the Balkan States.

During the period of the inflation, 1920-23, Austria was swamped with foreigners. It was hard to get a hotel. Workmen with a six shilling dole in England could live in a de luxe hotel for four shillings. One could buy an article for 100 cronin in the morning and sell it for 120 cronin in the afternoon.

---

[17] The number of Russian travelers staying at Viennese hotels in 1927 was less than one-eighth the number in 1912. See *Statistique Internationale des Grandes Villes*, p. 286.

Foreign currency brought in by tourists amounts to almost half of the trade balance deficit. In fact the tourist traffic is the biggest activity in Austria today (September, 1933). However, this traffic is not organic as in the United States, but artificial. The Opera, the University, musical schools and the Medical School have been kept open to attract tourists. Austria's first tourist bureau office was opened in London in 1926. In 1928 another was added in New York. We say, "Come to beautiful Austria" when we know it is not all beautiful. We say it is a cheap country, when we know it is really not cheap. We even advertise Austria in the Dutch Indies!

In 1927-29 de luxe hotels boomed. I was manager of the Ringstrasse at that time. The Wien Hotel, which has been in my family since 1841, did not feel the depression until 1931. The Ringstrasse felt it right away. The intellectual class, which patronizes the Wien, does not come any more. I received a letter recently from a librarian in Los Angeles saying that he could not come due to a cut in salary. Ninety per cent of the trade at the Wien are Anglo-Saxon *mental* types—English, American, Egyptian, Indian and Japanese.

Until the spring of 1933 more than half of the guest-nights in Austrian hotels were German. Since that time Hitler's edict requiring Germans to pay 1,000 marks for the privilege of entering Austria has cut this patronage to practically nothing. Many hotels have gone into bankruptcy. Eight hotels were offered for sale in Vienna last month (August, 1933), but there were no buyers.

The 1,000-mark rule sends Germans to Bavaria instead of to Austria, according to Professor Robert Glücksmann, director of the Research Institute for the Tourist Traffic in Berlin. The inland movement is good, but the *Ausländer* traffic is poor. There is a "See Germany" propaganda like the "See America First" slogan in the United States. Attractive posters in such places as railroad stations urge Germans to travel in the homeland. Government employees must spend their vacations in Germany. For most foreigners, on the other hand, Germany is an expensive country. The mark is stabilized, but the pound and dollar have dropped. The new government also makes people hesitate.

The energetic Berlin hotelkeeper, whose statements are given below, left his father's farm to begin his career as a busboy in a small town in Silesia. After serving as an apprentice here he was later employed in Swiss, Italian, French, Dutch, Belgian, Egyptian, Irish and English hotels. When he first came to Berlin in 1907 it was to help open an important hostelry on Unter den Linden. Vicki von Baum claims to have worked two weeks as a waitress in this hotel. It is said to be the scene for her *Menschen im Hotel* (People in the Hotel) which was later translated into English under the title *Grand Hotel*. The Herr Direktor von Schlesien likes the American film version, but when asked by the publisher for an opinion of the book he wrote: "The book *Menschen im Hotel* has not been written yet."

In 1907 and the years immediately following, Berlin was at its highest level. Everybody loved the German Emperor. In France they only had a president—a nobody. Delegates came to Berlin from Russia, Japan and China. Prince Tao Tsai came from China with a suite of forty-five people, not counting their Chinese cooks and men servants. They took over an entire floor in the hotel. Names on the doors were in Chinese and German. Today big men are always in a hurry. They look at the place a few days and then go on to some other city, perhaps Vienna or Paris. In former times they kept their apartments in Berlin while they visited Kiel and Essen. The big attraction, however, was the imperial court. Three different princes of Japan arrived in one day with their wives—guests of the Emperor. Waiters, taxi-drivers, laundresses, bakers, meat sellers, brewers, wine growers and theatres profit from such a situation. People in better-class hotels spend about twenty-five per cent for their hotel bill. This is especially true of wealthy young people. What they spend on a cabaret or other places makes the ten marks for a room look small.

Russians came to Berlin in large numbers before the war.[18] Grand dukes, big fur traders, timber dealers and great merchants hit Berlin first and just threw the money. All they had was money. There was a better night life in Berlin then than in Paris. Palais de Dance and Pavillon Mascotte were leading attractions. Paris was usually the next stop for Russians, then the Riviera and perhaps Cairo.

In the days before the Great War the Riviera was the farthest that most people thought of going. Today it is too near. Egypt is doing better because it is farther.

Americans were the hope of Germany to replace the Russian business, but the fall of the dollar has killed that trade. Now there is nothing.

Monsieur Joliet, who tells in the following interview about recent changes in the patronage of Parisian hotels, is one of the few hotel men who have the doctor's degree. He has been on his own since the age of thirteen. As a boy he worked in English hotels. Italians fought with knives in the basement. Waiters had to steal from the guests to get adequate food. He does not come from an aristocratic family. His father was a chef. Going into hotel work was not a thing that better-class parents would permit. It had little status at that time. At the present time M. Joliet owns one Parisian hotel and is the *directeur* of another. Both are first-class hostelries.

Before the war spring and autumn were the seasons in Paris. With the Grand Pris race in the Bois de Boulogne on July 1 the spring season ended. Soon after this event Paris was empty. In the autumn rich people came to Paris to buy clothes and de luxe articles. Russians were good patrons. Since winter in Paris is milder than in Russia, many people from that country spent the winter here. We still have a special bed which was made for the very tall Duke Nicolais. Because winter was the slack season, the Russians helped the hotel business.

Until 1914 many people came from America and England.

[18] 99,446 Russians stayed in Berlin hotels in 1912; 10,234, in 1927. *Ibid.*

The numbers were equal to, if not higher than, those at the present time (October, 1933). It was a different class, however, only rich people. In 1926-28 all kinds of Americans came. The numbers doubled. Now American travelers have been asking me to reduce prices according to the fall of the dollar. The cost of living is only a little less now than two years ago. Food has decreased in price ten per cent since 1930. Gas, electricity and water are the same.

The government levies taxes on the hotel industry for financial rather than economic purposes. It wants money and takes it without regard to the good of the industry. It thinks of the tax as a way of taking money from foreigners. Since 1917 the hotel tax has been on the basis of the *total income* of the hotel. Third-class hotels (I regret that your hotel is one of these) are taxed two per cent of the gross income; second-class hotels, three per cent; first-class, six per cent. There are forty first-class hotels in Paris. If they average one hundred rooms it would take 6,000 guests to fill them. That many rich people do not visit Paris. In fact a rich person is now an unusual sight. One wonders how he was able to save it. In the future capital will count less. Men will only live by the work they do. We entertained the Duke of Newcastle recently. The duke said he had to sell his castles. Fifty per cent of the income from his estates had been taken by the government.

The Paris of the past was a city of luxury. People came from all parts of the world to buy beautiful things. In the Paris of today the jewelry stores are especially hard hit.

M. Prevel, president of the National Hotel Association of France, told a special correspondent of the *New York Times* (April 6, 1934) that the business turnover in French hotels from 1930 to 1933 dropped 10 per cent in third-class hotels, from 30 to 50 per cent in second-class and from 50 to 75 per cent in hotels de luxe. The forty leading hotels of Paris, mentioned above, showed actual losses aggregating 46,000,-000 francs.

When habitats for travelers are considered from the standpoint of the areas in which they are located the following major types may be distinguished : (1) the transient hotel in the central business district, (2) the lodging house in the hobo areas, (3) the rooming house in the world of furnished rooms, and (4) the residential hotel in the more accessible residential neighborhoods. First-class hostelries and houses of ill-repute, Negro inns and Jewish hotels, small town houses and metropolitan caravanseries—all of these have characteristic locations.

The word "hotel" is sometimes used to include all types of habitats for travelers. The steamship, for example, has been described as a "floating hotel" and the pullman train as a "hotel on wheels." There is a growing feeling, however, that the term should be used more carefully. A club with its exclusive membership is not a hotel. Although the sanitorium has features in common with the resort hotel, it cares for the mentally or physically ill. The best American prisons with their short length of stay, wholesome food, recreational programs and radio in every cell approach the standards of a second-class hotel ; but the guests are not free to check out when they wish. The hotel is clearly different from the medieval inn or the present-day cottage court. The word "hotel" is frequently used—much to the disgust of "legitimate" hotel managers—over establishments that provide merely lodging or rooms. The better hotels provide food service as well as shelter service. The hotel in the narrower sense of that term, therefore, may be defined, very arbitrarily, as any house operated for profit which has not less than ten rooms available for transients, which charges a minimum price of fifty cents and which offers lodging to the general public.

CHAPTER IV

HOTEL HOMES

A VIVID CONTRAST to the modern American home is presented by the homestead of the pioneer. It was relatively self-sufficient, the scene of numerous activities. The house was frequently constructed of logs from the adjacent wood ; the rough furniture had a like origin. Food was either grown on the farm or procured by skill in hunting and fishing. All cooking was of course done at home. In this age of homespun every operation in the making of clothes, from sheep-shearing to sewing on buttons, was performed within the household.

A homestead in the Pacific Northwest, where some of the early pioneers are still living, will serve as an example.

Sixty-five years ago my grandparents arrived on timbered Puget Sound. Here they hewed for themselves a new home. Eventually there was a large ranch. On the rocky higher land, sheep, pigs, chickens, cows and horses were pastured. Draining into the bay, which bears their name, was a fertile valley where grain crops, a variety of orchard fruits, berries and vegetables were raised. Hay was often sold in sixty-ton shipments and home-made butter in one hundred pound lots. Such a ranch required the time of several hired men besides that of all of the eleven children who were old enough to work and still at home. The boys supplied the long table with venison, wild duck and geese. In the bay at the front door were clams, crabs and salmon. The only foodstuffs they bought for their abundant meals were sugar, flour, coffee, tea and spices. Machinery, seeds, boots and books were other important items of expenditure.

Although the parents had profited from medical and seminary

training, there was only a log school house for the children. On winter evenings, however, they gathered about the blazing logs in the big home fireplace while Grandfather read aloud from the best English literature to the accompaniment of the click-click from Grandmother's knitting needles. She knitted so many mittens, socks and sweaters from the wool of their own sheep that the children declare, "Mother's needles never ceased even when she fell asleep."

For many years neighborhood activities centered in this home. It was the postoffice, the library, a house of hospitality for the traveler, the Sunday school and the dispensary. Women came to do their sewing on the new Singer machine and, since the family also possessed an organ, the musical association met there on Saturday evenings.[1]

The economic independence of a family farm in the opposite corner of the country presents a similar picture.

During my childhood, which was passed on a rocky hillside farm in New England, farmers constituted a class more nearly independent than any other in the community. They produced nearly all the food that was necessary for their families. The owner of a small farm not infrequently raised corn, wheat, rye, barley, and buckwheat, as well as potatoes and all kinds of garden vegetables. The sweets for the table were often limited to the sugar and molasses that he made from the sap of the maple and to the honey collected by his bees.

Every farmhouse was a manufactory, not of one kind of goods, but of many. All day long in the chamber or attic the sound of the spinning-wheel and loom could be heard. Carpets, shawls, bedspreads, table-covers, towels, and cloth for garments were made from materials produced on the farm. The kitchen of the house was a baker's shop, a confectioner's establishment, and a chemist's laboratory. Every kind of food for immediate use was prepared there daily; and on special occasions sausages, head cheese, pickles, apple butter, and preserves were made. It was

---

[1] Una Middleton Hayner.

also the place where soap, candles, and vinegar were manufactured.[2]

Even the farm home of today reveals a very different pattern. Mail and the city newspaper are brought daily to the Rural Free Delivery box. A telephone affords easy contact with neighbors—sometimes too easy if a party line. A radio connects the home directly with the metropolitan broadcasting center. Electric lights replace the oil lamp and the candle. In the modern kitchen is a sink with running water and on the back porch stands an electric washing machine. An automobile and improved roads enable the smaller family of mechanized agriculture to choose groups on the basis of interest rather than proximity. The neighboring village or small town has become the marketing and recreational center. Production is more largely for sale than for sustenance. The home has, in fact, become part of the larger pecuniary society.

In small towns and cities the individual home is still the dominant form of family housing. Building-permit statistics indicate that new apartments were provided for only a little more than ten per cent of the families in independent cities with populations between 25,000 and 50,000. Smaller cities no doubt show smaller percentages. In spite of labor-saving devices there are still tasks in the separate house that are ordinarily allotted to the husband. There is the furnace to tend, the lawn to mow and perhaps a small garden to cultivate. Automatic furnaces are, however, increasing in number, back yards are becoming smaller, and gardens—with the exception of the depression variety—are less common. Generally speaking, smaller cities have a higher percentage of home ownership than larger cities. Tenancy also decreases as one moves outward from the metropolitan center to the

[2] Adapted from Rodney Welch, "The Farmer's Changed Condition," *Forum*, X (February, 1891), 689-91.

suburbs. The home-owning family in an outlying residential neighborhood moves so infrequently that it can scarcely avoid establishing roots in the community.

> I would rather hate to move. [Writes a student.] I know everyone who lives within a radius of four blocks, their troubles, misfortunes, their good luck. I go to see every new child that arrives. If one of the neighbors is ill, Mother visits her with a covered dish in her hand. She can stand for hours talking over the fence about her flowers. In the evenings when Papa mows the lawn he frequently stops for half an hour or so to talk with the captain across the street, who is usually mowing his lawn at the same time. I can close my eyes now and see Papa in his familiar pose, leaning on the handle of the lawn mower with his foot resting on one wheel, while the captain smokes one cigarette after another, talking all the while. I know I never could get used to another home. We are so much a part of our own particular neighborhood, that to move away would be like cutting a plant from its roots.

The home as contrasted with the hotel is a place of permanent abode. Home life is commonly associated with hearth and fireside, wife and children, rather than with movement, bright lights and a free and detached existence. Partly because of this fact it has become enshrined in sentiment and affection.

> "Mid pleasures and palaces though we may roam,
>   Be it ever so humble there's no place like home."

Living in one place seems to be a prerequisite for the development of those habits and sentiments—that body of tradition—graphically described by Edgar Guest as a "Heap o' Livin'."

> "Home ain't a place that gold can buy or get up
>   in a minute;
>   Afore it's home there's got to be a heap o' livin'
>   in it."

The joys and sorrows of life must be identified with the house to make it home.

Unless you sacrifice and plan, and scheme to improve your house; unless you work on or about it yourselves; unless you plant a shrub or a flower and watch and work over it to make it a success; unless you scheme and plan and dream over your place until it becomes a part of your soul, it will never be a real home to you.[3]

Two major trends may be distinguished in urban residential housing: one, the suburban, is outward; the other, toward multiple dwellings, is upward. The suburban movement seems to be composed largely of families with children who prefer the greater elbow room of life in an individual home. Within the larger cities, however, the long-time trend is definitely toward multiple dwellings and wholesale housekeeping. During the period from 1921 to 1928 the percentage of urban families provided for in new one-family dwellings dropped from 58.3 to 35.2. The percentage provided for in new multifamily dwellings during the same period climbed from 24.4 to 53.7.[4] In 1929 and 1930, to be sure, the percentage for one-family dwellings rose again to 45.7, but this was probably only a temporary depression phenomenon. The apartment house is essentially an investment property and investors are quick to adjust their plans to fundamental changes in economic conditions.

It is especially in metropolitan cities that habits of life are being changed by apartments. Not only are metropolites living more and more in multiple dwellings, but the average size of these structures has increased. In the last few years several skyscraper apartments have been built. These "residential cities" have been located near the central business

---

[3] E. T. Meredith, publisher and managing editor of *Fruit, Garden and Home*, July, 1923, p. 3.

[4] United States Bureau of Labor Statistics, *Building Permits in the Principal Cities of the United States in 1928*, p. 4.

districts of New York and Chicago. They answer the desire of business and professional people to live near their work. Since they cater to higher income groups they are able to compete with business for high-land-value sites.[5]

As the multiple house has become larger, the "family dwelling unit" has decreased in size. The Regional Survey of New York reports that in 1913 the average number of rooms in apartments was 4.19; in 1928, 3.34. The high cost of space has reduced the kitchen to the kitchenette or 'mixing closet'; the dining room to a mere breakfast nook; and the bedroom to an in-a-door bed. This last invention, appearing first in San Francisco, has spread from the West through the East. "Everything is collapsible, sliding, folding, built-in, grooved or hung on pivots."[6] "The family no longer dwells; it occupies quarters."[7]

With the automobile at the curb, the home needs to be less a place to live in because it is so easy to get away from. There is more temptation to be always on the go and home becomes merely an over-night parking place for the few hours after we finish our evening's entertainment and before the working part of the family must report at its place of earning its daily bread.[8]

Under the conditions of modern city life the "heap o' livin' " prerequisite to the establishment of a "real home" is difficult, and in many cases impossible to attain. The shift from a household to a factory economy is a basic factor in this urban decline in home life. Numerous activities that were characteristic of the pioneer homestead have been gradually transferred to industry. The manufacture of met-

[5] See McKenzie, *op. cit.*, pp. 217-20 and 222-23.

[6] Miriam Beard, "New York Squeezes Into the 'Domestic Unit,' " *New York Times Magazine*, November 7, 1926.

[7] Edward Sapir, "What is the Family Still Good For?" *American Mercury*, XIX (February, 1930), 146.

[8] John F. Harrison, "The Automobile and the Home of the Future," *The Annals of the American Academy of Political and Social Science*, CXVI (November, 1924), 58.

als, implements and furniture, spinning and weaving; the making of clothing; the preparation of medicines and soap —these activities were lost in the order named. More recently there has been a decline in the extent to which foods are prepared in the home. Between 1900 and 1920 the number of waiters increased about three times as fast as the population and the number of restaurant keepers about four times as fast. Between 1910 and 1920 the number of delicatessen shops grew about three times as rapidly as the number of families. Only about one per cent of urban homes use home-made bread exclusively.[9] The housewife today is frequently accused of "cooking with a can opener."

THE RESIDENTIAL HOTEL

Hotel homes are not without precedent in the past. Only the wealthy residents of ancient Rome lived in separate houses. The mass of the population ate and slept in what were called *insulae*, or islands, because they were surrounded on all sides by streets. These Roman "rabbit-warrens" seem to have been more like our present-day rooming houses than like hotels. At least they did not encourage "that simple, sacred family life which had once been the ethical basis of Roman society." Some of the most respectable of the *meritoria* of ancient Rome were perhaps more similar to our modern family hotels.[10]

Many "substitutes for the home" are described by Henry Shelley in *Inns and Taverns of Old London.* Coffee houses, clubs and pleasure-gardens, as well as inns and taverns, were among them. Washington Irving describes a residential hotel in Paris in 1825 as "rather a quiet, retired hotel, where most

---

[9] See William F. Ogburn, "The Family and Its Functions" in *Recent Social Trends* (2 vols., New York, 1933), I, 661-708—also "The Changing Family," *Publications of the American Sociological Society*, XXIII (1928), 124-33.

[10] See Firebaugh, *op. cit.*, p. 242 and W. Warde Fowler, *Social Life at Rome in the Age of Cicero* (New York, 1909), pp. 28-29.

of the inmates are permanent residents from year to year, so that there is more of the spirit of neighborhood, than in the bustling, fashionable hotels in the gay parts of Paris which are continually changing their inhabitants."[11] There were practically no one-family dwellings in Vienna until the Social Democrats recently built several large areas of them as a small part of their huge housing achievement for about 200,000 working-class people.

In the United States hotel and boarding house life have attracted attention and excited comment since about 1830.

Young married people constituted a large part of the clientele of the boarding establishments. The life was livelier than could be found in the seclusion of a home, and attracted young women still in giddy girlhood. It was a comfort to have no housework or other duties ; plenty of time was available for amusements. This careless public existence often continued from a couple's youth to their maturity and might even be resumed after a period of housekeeping.

In hotels and boarding-houses women were free to gossip and, having nothing else to do, were prone to enjoy the freedom. What should have been family secrets became public property, and differences between husband and wife were complicated by the "sympathy" of meddlesome onlookers.

What F. A. Walker calls "the vice of boarding" was correlated with the great social and industrial changes following 1850 : manufactures, commerce, city growth, gold discovery, increasing distinction between extremes of wealth and poverty, the reign of fashion and luxury. The rise of house rent after the Civil War, the difficulty of the servant problem, the instability of employment, all counted against the establishment of homes. Families of moderate means were able to make a bigger show on a small income, to secure more conveniences and social facilities, and a better table.[12]

[11] *The Works of Washington Irving* (23 vols., New York, 1865-1867), XVI, 195.

[12] Adapted from Arthur W. Calhoun, *A Social History of the American Family* (3 vols., Cleveland, 1917-1919), II, 238-41 and III, 179-82.

The boarding house is increasingly a thing of the past in the modern American city. As urbanization sets in, the restaurant takes over its food service and the rooming house supplies its shelter service. These specialized institutions are much more impersonal and less homelike than the old-fashioned boarding house.

Boarders knew each other, they met at table two or three times a day, and lingered a few moments in conversation after dinner in the evening. In summer they gathered on the front steps and piazzas, and in winter they often played euchre and whist in the landlady's parlor. Congenial temperaments had a chance to find each other. There was a public parlor in which guests were received and, in a reputable boarding-house at least, a girl would not have thought of taking a gentleman caller to her own room. The landlady of a good boarding-house took something of a personal interest, even if remote, in her boarders, and they often found themselves becoming a part of the family even against their wills. There was a certain personal element in the relations between individuals; no one could be isolated and entirely shut up within himself.[13]

Permanent guests in hotels are much more unusual on the continent of Europe than in the United States. The hotel is regarded as a place to stay for only a short time. To a certain extent the pension takes the place of the residential hotel. This is really a boarding house. There are two popular arrangements: (1) room and breakfast known as half pension and (2) room with all meals known as full pension. The former is increasingly preferred by natives. Although guests are taken for one or a few days, particularly in depression times, a special rate is usually given for those staying five days or so. Many young couples have moved into pensions since the war. The big motive is to escape taxes.

Life in the continental pension is much like that in the older type of American boarding house. Guests get ac-

---

[13] A. B. Wolfe, *The Lodging House Problem in Boston*, pp. 46-47.

quainted at the leisurely meal times. The frequent differences in nationality backgrounds make the patrons especially interesting to each other. The proprietor is usually a host in the true sense of that term.

The guests we met in the dining room of a Viennese pension were both engaging and friendly. Perhaps the exquisite radio music from an adjacent drawing room helped. There was the portly gray-haired gentleman from German-speaking Switzerland who told us every evening about some new *Bierkeller* he had discovered. Next to him sat an elderly Jewish shopkeeper who had dined at this pension for the two years since his wife's death. Then there was the lady who came to Vienna for a few weeks each year to shop and visit with friends. This year she was also going to Budapest. A young Pole, down for a month's good time, was enthusiastic about Vienna's Coney Island, the amusement park in the Prater.

More reticent at first than the others was an attractive young American woman. Three years before she had married a Lithuanian engineering professor. He had just been sent to Russia on a dangerous mission and in his absence she had come down to Vienna alone for medical help. She was worried about her husband's safety, may have been concerned about her own health and was homesick for the States. The winter before she had paid sixty cents a pound in Lithuania for Wenatchee apples.

One evening in September 1933 the proprietress of our pension, a poised and cultured hostess, summed up the attitudes of many Viennese by saying: "Most of us are for Hitler. Austria is in an impossible situation. She cannot go on. She is down. She must go in with some other country. I hope it will be Germany."[14]

Monsieur Joliet[15] thinks that Parisians will live in hotels more in the future.

The French are very much attached to their furniture which has often been inherited from ancestors. They want a home.

---

[14] Una Middleton Hayner.
[15] See chap. III.

My mother at the age of 76 has a good income from rents, but not for a fortune would she move to a hotel. When the children come home she wants to be at the head of the table. In France the lady who is not married is not a lady. The girl who is not married does not vote. A lady seldom travels alone. Practically all women guests in hotels are with their husbands. The ideal for girls is different. They are brought up to be housewives. In New York I was surprised to meet girls who could talk politics and swim, but knew little about taking care of a house. The French like the personal touch and hotels are impersonal. They like the poetry of life. They love tradition. Nevertheless the size of apartments in Paris has been cut as in the United States. Many Parisians live in one room and kitchenette. Residential hotels are coming.

The manager of the famous London hostelry where Arnold Bennett is said to have gotten ideas for his *Imperial Palace,* stated in an interview that home life is also very strong in England.

Small private houses are greatly in demand in London. The Englishman likes to have his own front door. The man who flits about—Monte Carlo, New York, South Africa—likes the flat. The well-to-do find themselves too crowded in flats and search for small private houses. Servants are easier to get in England than in America. Cheap blocks of flats go, but when they are high they do not sell. Blocks of flats are also available with restaurants. Most residential hotels operate on what is called the American plan in the United States, i.e., a combined rate for room and meals.

In spite of the strength of home life the Registrar-General reported 5,277 residential hotels for England and Wales in 1921. 132,501 persons, or one for every three hundred in the total population, lived in these hotels. The proportion must have been higher in the cities. In fact as long ago as 1916, W. L. George commented on the trend toward hotel living.

All over the center of London, in Piccadilly, along Hyde Park, in Bloomsbury, hotels have risen—the Piccadilly, the new Ritz, the Park View, the Coburg, the Cadogan, the Waldorf, the Jermyn Court, the Marble Arch, so many that in some places they are beginning to form a row. And still they rise. An enormous hotel is being built opposite Green Park; another is projected at Hyde Park corner; the Strand Palace is open, and at the Regent Palace there are, I understand, fourteen hundred bedrooms. The position is that a proportion of London's population is beginning to live in these hotels without servants of their own, without furniture of their own, without houses of their own. A more detached, a freer spirit is invading them, and a desire to get all they can out of life, while they can, instead of solemnly worshipping the Englishman's castle.[16]

Not far from the British Museum is a rather antiquated but moderately priced residential hotel that is probably typical of the best houses of its class. The floor shakes when walked on and there is no central heating; but the manager speaks both French and German, was for years director of one of the finest restaurants in London, and buys all his food personally. Since almost a fourth of his gross revenue must go to the government, even a man of his training can barely make a go of it in hard times. The following experience gives a picture of life in this hotel.

London fogs are chill and raw in November and they penetrate indoors. But when I think of the residential hotel near Russell Square where we spent three weeks I think of warmth, coziness, friendliness.

The establishment was, to be sure, rather out-of-date. A row of residences one hundred and fifty years old had been remodeled so that hallways pierced the walls that once separated them. Modern plumbing had been installed and electric wiring had been added on top of the plaster, but our spacious room possessed only a small gas heater. A penny in the slot every half hour

---

[16] "The Downfall of the Home," *Harper's*, CXXX (June, 1916), 57.

served to moderate the chilliness. Hot water bottles were placed in the beds at night if desired. Still we liked the place.

Just behind the hotel, cathedral bells pealed musically each quarter hour. There was an excellent dining service—remarkable for England. There was also a friendly atmosphere in the lounge as the older guests gathered around the hearth-fires after dinner. For entertainment there was the interesting government-controlled radio with its world news and no advertising. Some of the guests read, some wrote letters, there was a little conversation and occasionally a card game. A crochety old couple always found chairs in the same corner where they watched those around them with interest and bickered with each other. Shortly after nine o'clock the wife would rave and ring because James never did remember to bring the milk and medicine on time.[17]

An American girl, who traveled for more than four years with Pavlowa's Ballet Russe through South America, Europe and the United States describes in an unpublished paper differences in her treatment as a visitor in these cultural settings.

South American hotels were mostly of the summer resort type with huge verandas, large halls and airy bedrooms—sometimes with bath or shower. In the little town of Quayaquil, Ecuador, near the equator, three days of frequent shower baths drained the water supply and the management had to dig up the street in front of the hotel to sink another well. In London we lived in a little "private hotel" where we met all the guests—mostly English women alone in the world who found more pleasure in a well-run place of this kind than in an apartment. Everyone, except the girls in our troupe, who were too busy, gathered about the fireplace in the living room after dinner and read or played cards. In the United States hotel life seemed very commercial and business-like and we never felt safe unless the doors were locked. Here we never met anyone in a single hotel.

The large size of many American hotels, especially those located in the big cities, is an important factor in making

---

[17] Una Middleton Hayner.

them impersonal. In general the more permanent the residents and the smaller the dwelling, the more intimate and personal are the relationships; the more transient the population and the larger the house, the more relations tend to be casual and impersonal. In the large metropolitan hostelry, hotel service is a great enterprise and includes almost all the professional and commercial activities of a small but high-grade business district. A broker, chiropodist, dentist, florist, house physician and hospital, jewelry shop, photographer, public stenographic bureau and Turkish baths are only part of this service. Occasionally a daily newspaper is published for the guests. Under these circumstances the desire, that every normal human being has, to be recognized as a distinct personality—to be known to the members of a group and have a place in it—seems to be a force driving the guest to the greater warmth and sociability of the smaller hotel. The manager of one of these huge houses of hospitality in New York City has noticed a tendency on the part of those patrons who have been in the city some time to move to smaller apartment and family hotels.

The glamour of big palaces attracts temporarily, but in time there is a longing to get into places where one may be known, may be a personality, a guest in the true sense of the word.[18]

The significant fact about a small home-like residential hotel such as the one described below is that the residents know each other better than in a larger hotel. Of course the "old tabbies" in a quasi-boarding house of this kind know far less about the residents than the average village gossip, but on the other hand they know far more than the gossips of a larger hostelry.

---

[18] "Ye Genial Host" by a Hotel Man, *Saturday Evening Post*, April 1, 1922. "On the average the new hotels which have been built are larger than those commonly built prior to 1920," wrote E. M. Statler in *Nation's Business* for June, 1928.

The Pioneer was once a large private home occupied by one of the first settlers in the community but it has been remodeled so that it now has the traditional hotel lobby and dining room. An addition in the rear makes a total of 54 rooms, accommodating ninety-five guests. There are many school teachers, students and stenographers among the residents. About one-third of the population are elderly persons. All are permanent in the sense that they stay a month or more. A writer has lived in this hotel thirteen years. She complains of the "noise and confusion" in the lobby and hallways and now has a room on the third and top floor, but here the servants, away from the watchful eye of the housekeeper, enjoy frequent conversations under the open transom of her room. Gossip is an important activity here and each guest is carefully watched by certain "old tabbies" who inhabit the place. "If you want to spoil a good disposition, live in a small hotel," she says.

Relationships are much more casual and impersonal in the large transient hostelry than in the small residential hotel. In the latter the manager probably knows his guests by name and is familiar with their individual needs and peculiarities. Life is sometimes compared with that in a small town. But the manager of a large metropolitan hotel rarely meets his guests. Human relations here are distinctly urban. It is interesting in this connection that the better-class hotels in the United States are almost uniformly larger than ordinary hotels. These hotels have a superior type of construction and are built where labor costs are higher. They also provide more public space and offer more services. According to data compiled by Horwath and Horwath and published in the 1928 edition of the Hotel Red Book the number of employees per 100 rooms, the annual sales per room and the investment per room increase consistently as the size of the hotel increases. Hotels over 1,000 rooms had more than three times as many employees per 100 rooms as hotels with less than 50 rooms. They also had more than ten times the annual sales and more than six times the investment per room.

J. O. Dahl, managing director of the Ahrens Publications, thinks that "New York families of moderate or better financial circumstances" have preferred consecutively the following ways of living:

First, of course, there were private detached houses and practically nothing else. Then came the brownstone front—sometimes a two-family affair. Then "flats" appeared. They gradually went up in the social scale and became apartments. Then, because of economic advantages—real or fancied—the coöperative apartment made its bow. Finally we have developed apartment hotels and they will rapidly come into their own as the "new way of living."[19]

There seems to be a definite ratio between land values and the number of people who move to hotels. The land occupied by apartment buildings is on the whole more valuable than that occupied by individual homes. It is therefore a more costly undertaking to maintain a private house in an apartment area. Taxes are prohibitive. As transportation facilities improve and mobility of population increases, there seems to be a point at which land also becomes too valuable for the ordinary three or four story apartment house. This form of housing in turn tends to be replaced by larger apartment buildings, apartment hotels, residential hotels, transient hotels, or even by a new kind of utility such as theatres, business buildings or shops. And of course the building of apartment houses in an area of single residences or of hotels in an apartment house area increases the land values. To home lovers it is a vicious circle.

The apartment hotel differs from the apartment house in

---

[19] From the Introduction by J. O. Dahl to *Housekeeping Management in Hotels and Institutions* (New York, 1931) by his wife, Crete M. Dahl, p. viii. Central rather than separate heating is sometimes used as the distinction between apartments and flats.

that it offers hotel service of various kinds in addition to the provision of living quarters. As Lucius M. Boomer, president of the Waldorf-Astoria Corporation, points out below, the apartment hotel also differs considerably from the commercial house.

Formerly, residential hotels did not differ greatly in layout, appointments and service features from the high type of transient hotels. Today, there is a rapidly growing number of apartment hotels, specially designed and equipped for residential purposes, and quite unsuitable for taking care of transients advantageously. The modern residential hotels consist of suites that may be rented furnished or unfurnished, often equipped with kitchen or kitchenettes. A suite may have the spaciousness and luxurious appointments of an elaborate private residence. Most of these hotels maintain restaurants, and if a tenant desires, personal laundry service, in fact all the numerous services common to transient hotels are provided for tenants.[20]

A statistical study of fifty large apartment hotels conducted by *Hotel Management* showed an average of fourteen per cent of the rooms listed as transient. The ratio of furnished apartments to unfurnished was two to one. Due to limited turnover the average occupancy percentage (87.3 in 1929) was markedly higher than for comparable transient houses. James S. Warren, editor of the magazine, concludes: "Just as surely as the trend developed away from the private home and toward the apartment house, so will the ultimate step be away from the apartment house and toward the apartment hotel."[21]

---

[20] *Hotel Management*, pp. 5-6. In his foreword to the second edition of this book (1931) Mr. Boomer directs attention to "the noteworthy tendency of thousands of people to make modern hotels their city *homes*. . . . An increasing number of people have country or shore homes. They cannot afford or do not desire to maintain a town house and a country house, too, but for business and social reasons they do desire to be in town frequently and for extended periods."

[21] "What the Typical Apartment Hotel 'Looks Like,' " November, 1930, pp. 406-8.

Sometimes an attempt is made to differentiate apartment and residential hotels. The residential hotel in the restricted use of that term does not provide cooking facilities in its individual rooms or suites. The apartment hotel usually installs kitchenettes for this purpose. Residential hotels also commonly offer only furnished quarters. The 1930 Hotel Census included residential hotels but excluded apartment hotels. The latter were apparently considered more akin to apartments than to hotels. In the United States as a whole, according to this census, the number of guest rooms mainly permanent totaled about one-third of those mainly transient. In Chicago and New York the number in these two categories were approximately equal. In San Francisco there were four times as many mainly permanent rooms as mainly transient. It is obvious that the number of permanent rooms would be much larger if apartment hotels were also included.

It is a mistake to think that the persons who occupy these permanent rooms are really permanent, however. The people who live in the better-class residential hotels in Chicago, for example, travel a great deal and frequently spend the different seasons at various resorts. Many will remain in their hotel homes until after the opera season, i.e., until February, and then leave for Florida or Southern California. Even more leave the city in June or thereabouts for widely scattered summer "watering places," only to have their places taken by vacationists from the too sunny South. Guests seldom live in a hotel the year round. There are so few who do so that they are well known and remarked about. In one large residential hotel the annual range of guests is said to be all over the world. There are people in China and in Europe, who, although they may not have a suite of rooms at the time, look upon this hotel as their home.

CHAPTER V

WHY LIVE IN A HOTEL?

FREEDOM TO DO as one wishes is the most appealing and the most dangerous of the four reasons why people make their homes in hotels rather than in apartments or separate houses. "You are in a position to spend your time exactly as you wish," writes the enthusiastic hotel man. This freedom enables real contributions to the world of business, science, art or literature. It also leads to personal disorganization and social waste.

Because it is miscellaneous and repetitious in character the statement has been made that "housework seems to rot the mind." Living in a hotel affords a means of escape. "Here you have no housekeeping cares and troubles," the promotor argues. Even in the apartment hotels the management takes over every burden for its patrons except cooking the food and washing the dishes. Kitchenette floors are scrubbed; sinks, ice-boxes and cupboards, scoured. Guests can have a home and yet be spared many of the difficulties associated with maintaining a house. As Mr. Boomer has pointed out in his book on *Hotel Management:* "Fundamentally a hotel is a domestic establishment run for profit."

Under the conditions of life in large cities the big private home is becoming more and more the rich man's privilege. Fifteen or more rooms to keep in order, a generous lawn with perhaps a garden to care for, a furnace to struggle with in winter, meals to be cooked, dishes to be washed, children to be supervised—all these, together with the growing number of demands for time outside of the home, make servants a necessity. But it is difficult to get satisfactory servants for private dwellings. Factories compete with housekeepers and wages rise. Domestics are more particular about "hours and conditions" and demand more freedom than in the "good old days" when a maid could be had for $2.50 a week and keep. Although good servants can still be hired in Europe, immigration has been restricted since the war and foreign girls already here have become Americanized. This has usually meant the abandonment of housework for something more satisfying.

Experiences such as those described below lead many people to "pass the buck" to the hotel man and "let him worry about it."

Until her two daughters were grown, Dr. Caroline Williams lived in an individual house. She hired a man to care for the furnace and lawn, and a maid to help inside. Here there was opportunity for self-expression, but there was also a great deal of responsibility. When the sink was stopped up she had to call a plumber. If she wanted to entertain, she must secure the co-operation of the maid.

Shortly after she moved to an apartment, the daughters married. She found less responsibility in the apartment, but at one time she had to push the janitor's baby about in order to get his wife to scrub her kitchen floor! The maid was a college girl and couldn't see such work; the janitor thought it was unmanly, and his wife did it only under protest. The janitor did condescend to unplug the kitchen sink as well as care for the furnace, however.

Three years ago last October she moved to the Ritz Hotel. She had been living alone in the apartment while the son was away and when he decided to stay in New York, she moved to the hotel. Here there was total loss of responsibility. When a storm blew up during her absence, she never worried about rain coming in the open windows, for she knew someone had closed them. She could be as aloof from the world as in the woods and yet have sociability if desired, either by phone or on the mezzanine floor.

The following paragraphs from a paper entitled "Two Years in a Residential Hotel" were written by the daughter of a Chicago banker. They not only explain why her family moved to a suburban hotel, but also suggest a gradual accommodation or adjustment to the new way of living.

A year or two before we moved into the Lakeview Hotel, we would have scoffed the very idea of our ever living any place but in our own home, but time brings great changes, and before we knew it two of my sisters were married, one was teaching away from home, and my brother was in training camp. We realized that as long as our family was exactly cut in half, the burdens of a large home were too much for such a small family to shoulder. So we were soon established in a residential hotel in a beautiful suburb of Chicago. For persons accustomed to the spaciousness of a home, the shut-in feeling of our rooms was not pleasant, but as we became acquainted with our neighbors, we accustomed ourselves to the different life and it no longer seemed strange.

We found numerous types of people living together under this one roof, and some appeared very strange to my young and inexperienced eyes. There were many business men living there, both single and married, all of whom were commuters, preferring to live in the clean suburban town than in the busy hurried city. One of our friends, a bachelor, found the Lakeview Hotel the most desirable along the North Shore because he wanted to feel he would be in an entirely different atmosphere as soon as he left Chicago and his business. Also he had in this suburb many friends who kept his spare time busy.

Besides the business man we also found the business woman. Those lone women said this suburban hotel was much more to their liking than a larger, more commercial one in the city for it offered safer living and a friendlier, more unquestioning environment. One woman moved to the hotel with her young daughter many years ago, after some domestic difficulty. For financial reasons she was obliged to take up some profession, and now is a very successful doctor. Her daughter is grown and is soon to be married, but Dr. Saunders will continue to live at the hotel because she finds, as she has no domestic duties, her time, when not devoted to her patients, is absolutely her own and she is free to go and come as she pleases.

People who are alone in the world—the divorced, the widowed, the single—frequently find their most satisfactory home in a hotel. Some, like Dr. Caroline Williams, have maintained establishments of their own; others have been merely roomers in private residences.

My last experience in a private family drove me to a hotel and now I think it would be impossible to live in a home again. The family from whom I rented a room were inquisitive and prying. I'm sure they investigated my room during my absence. The bathroom was occupied for prolonged periods, and last but not least, they seemed to think I should remain with them for the rest of my life. My relief was great the day I left with bag and baggage and moved into a hotel. No matter how secluded one keeps in a private family, if the members don't ask questions directly they are conjecturing among themselves. They know exactly the time one returns home, of what one's personal effects consist, the status of one's friends. In a hotel all this is avoided. After a day of hard work it is a comfort to return home without having to meet inquisitive or talkative people in whom one is not especially interested. If one wishes to move furniture, change pictures, entertain guests, there is nothing to interfere. This gives a feeling of stability. This may sound laughable to a person who is living in his own family but nevertheless my hotel apartment gives me that feeling. I can come home in the afternoon, make a cup of tea or have a nap before dinner.

Tending to form a circle around the central business district in any large American city are areas where the commercial land values are high and the rents for residential purposes low. Industry has not yet taken possession but is near enough to make the district undesirable as a place in which to live. Here slums develop and the poor and vicious congregate. As the central business and industrial district expands, neighborhoods that were at one time first-class residential areas disintegrate and those families that can move out usually do so.

Mr. and Mrs. Thomas lived in an eleven-room house on Michigan Avenue for thirty-four years. Their neighborhood was at one time a first-class residential district. Many respectable people lived there including, among others, the president of a railroad. Slowly the community deteriorated until the police would occasionally knock on the door, contemplating a raid, mistaking their home for the house next door which was disorderly. Finally they moved to the Southshore Hotel. Until recently they were dissatisfied but now the son thinks they will never go back to housekeeping. Mrs. Thomas enjoys the freedom that enables her to attend concerts, lectures and the theatre—pleasures which had previously been curtailed by the responsibility of maintaining a large home.

Closely related to this freedom from responsibility, which makes a larger portion of the guest's time available for "matters of moment," is the *convenience* of hotel life. A location near the business center, for example, appeals both to people who wish to live close to the places where they are employed and to those who like easy access to the shopping district.

For twenty-five years or more Mr. and Mrs. Martin had lived in their own individual home in a small industrial city of Illinois. Later they had lived for twenty-one years in various Chicago apartments. Their one child, a daughter, married before they moved to the hotel where they had previously been in the habit of taking their dinners. Mrs. Martin believes that if it were not for the greater expense when entertaining guests, living in a hotel would be more reasonable than in an apartment.

Although she enjoyed her own home, she "could not bear the thought" of returning to it. She likes to be in the center of things, revels in a crowd, and appreciates being near the shopping district, for she shops in the Loop stores practically every morning.

Her husband teases her by saying that he expects to find her cot in front of Marshall Field's some morning! She enjoyed dancing until two years ago when she "broke" her foot, and every evening in the dining room, even now, her feet keep time with the orchestra. She spends many happy hours in her room sewing for her nieces and other relatives. "This is my life here," she said referring to the hotel. "I shall never return to my own home."

Because of the small size of modern city apartments it is more difficult to provide for Grandmother than it was in the individual homes of former days. There is no quiet corner to which she may retire, and there are fewer tasks that she may share. The hotel offers modern grandparents, like Mr. and Mrs. Martin, comfort and independence. An increasing number of elderly people are spending their declining years in hotel homes.

School teachers also enjoy the comfort and convenience of hotel life. In one of Seattle's large downtown hotels, for example, sixty per cent of the guests were found to be women, and fifty-five, or about fourteen per cent of the total house count, were teachers. One of these schoolma'ams, who has lived in Seattle hotels about ten years, stated the matter thus : "When a woman has taught all day and disciplined forty-odd lively children she wants to go home to a room or apartment far above the street level, where there's lots of heat and hot water and no noise." The experience of another representative of the fifty-five is pictured in the statement below.

Previous to moving here I had lived in an apartment with a stenographer. Finally she decided to stay with friends. We had become tired of each other's company and I was more than tired of her beau. In the hotel I can entertain my friends without feeling that they are not wanted. I do not have to take care of the room. I have four towels each day, fresh sheets several times a week, hot water at any hour, lots of light and heat and a private bath. In the hotel are a restaurant, laundry, dry cleaning establishment, bootblack and many mail deliveries a day. The management does not object to the use of electrical appliances so I have a grill, iron and percolator.

Especially in the minds of feminine guests, the *protection* afforded by the present-day hotel is an important factor. Seldom does a modern fireproof hostelry burn. In regions visited by earthquakes the leading hotels are also built to resist shocks. A watchman patrols the halls at intervals during the night. Men who must be away from home overnight or for long periods usually have a feeling of security when they leave their wives or mothers in a hotel rather than alone in a large house. There are always people near in case of difficulty, and in the smaller and more intimate places, the opportunity for sociability may prevent lonesomeness during the absence.

The protection which the better hotels provide against insurance salesmen, community fund solicitors and student investigators may be a loss to the community, but it is a distinct advantage from the standpoint of the hotel dweller. Residents expect the management to guarantee the utmost in privacy. They can leave word at the desk that they do not wish to be disturbed either by telephone or by visitors. The average guest is individualistic, self-concerned and not interested in social welfare. Any attempt at personal contact by strangers or even by members of the hotel staff, except in their official capacity, is not tolerated. The manager is merely a person to whom complaints or criticisms are to be made. Assurance of privacy to the guest seems to be both an essential doctrine for successful hotelkeeping and also an important reason for living in a hotel.

Managers and guests agree that it is *cheaper* for a city family of considerable income—say eight thousand dollars a year, or more—to live in a hotel than in a large home of its own. Until the White House called them, President and

Mrs. Coolidge had never maintained a home in Washington other than a modest apartment in a downtown hotel—the same one occupied during the whole of the second term of his office by Vice-President and Mrs. Marshall.

Here they held receptions, received their guests, at rather few and modest dinner parties, and entertained guests from out of town. It is at the northeast corner of the fourth floor of the Willard, famous for many generations as a home for politicians and officials.

There was an effort for a pretentious vice-presidential home made last season by Mrs. John B. Henderson, houser of foreign diplomats, but this effort was quelled quickly by the Vice President himself, who said it was out of the question to maintain such a residence on a $12,000 a year salary.[1]

There is no such clear-cut agreement on the comparative expense of apartment and hotel. It will be recalled that Mrs. Martin, in the interview recorded above, found that the cost of entertaining friends was the item that made the hotel less reasonable than the flat. A successful business man of the same city believes that the hotel is cheaper.

My chief reason in going to a hotel was the difficulty in getting competent household labor. Until about 1917 I had no trouble with servants—could get good ones at a price I could afford to pay. After my marriage I lived four years in an eight-room apartment, seventeen years in a large twelve-room house, one year in a hotel and about a year ago I rented another apartment. When the lease on my apartment expires in September I intend to return to some hotel. I believe that all in all it is cheaper to live in a hotel than in an apartment of reasonable size. I know that it is cheaper in a hotel than in a large house. However, I do not have in an apartment, and especially in a hotel, that feeling of permanence and of being at home that I had in a house.

---

[1] *Chicago Tribune*, August 4, 1923. "The four outstanding luxury hotels of New York," writes a hotel man, "are today (December 18, 1934) pretty well filled with people who could formerly keep up a house."

Other guests lament with this business man the absence in the hotel of that "feeling of permanence and of being at home" that they had in their own houses. Some of them seriously question the advantages of hotel life—its freedom, convenience, protection and smaller expense. This was true of the mother and daughter whose attitudes are given below. When the father died they moved from their individual home to an apartment. Here they lived for nine years, until a hotel structure began to rise next door. The noise of the automatic hammers at work on the steel framework of this building finally forced them to sublet the apartment and seek a quieter residence in a hotel home.

To the mother, hotel life involved a loss of responsibility.

You have the same feeling as on an ocean liner. You are disconnected and have no sense of community. There are no opportunities for services—no chance to do the little tasks for other members of the family. These are all done for you.

The daughter felt that she could not express herself. There was no manual labor to perform. The hotel furniture, hangings, rugs and room-service china were not of her choice. Only in pictures could she "express her personality."

Not infrequently we awake with depression because we are here. Mother is, I think, sufficiently disturbed by it to be somewhat affected in health. She has told me at least a hundred times why we had to leave the apartment. When I have these moments of dejection over the situation I try to see the absurdity of it, considering the comfort and ease. I remember French refugees and all the homelessness in Europe, Diogenes in his tub, the Czarina of Russia in a box car and my grandfather, who was in a Libby Prison coal hole for thirty-seven days. I see the folly of my attitude but the discontent remains to crop up into consciousness in leisure moments. And why? How would a day of leisure and no engagements have been different in my own home?

In my apartment I should have been surrounded by things which meant something to me—something beautiful or pleasant.

In such surroundings, as in a lovely garden, there is a touch of affection that warms the heart. Here there is practically nothing which pleases the eye or which has happy associations. I am surrounded by alien things. At home I should have had some housework and should very likely have asked a friend in for lunch or dinner. Here there is not the same pleasure in entertaining, partly because of the expense and partly because I give less enjoyment. A day of being busy elsewhere is the only endurable kind to have in a hotel.

PART II

PEOPLE WHO LIVE IN HOTELS

CHAPTER VI

TRENDS IN THE HOTEL POPULATION

Mr. Jefferson Williamson in his interesting anecdotal history of *The American Hotel* states that there was throughout the nineteenth century "no such universality of touring and tripping and vacationing as there is today." People of every class, especially the poor, traveled less than they do now. Travel for its own sake was as yet unimportant. Furthermore the hotel population was predominantly masculine.

The twentieth century has seen the development of a new family toy which has put many persons on the gipsy trail who formerly did not think of traveling. The American Automobile Association estimates that about 40,000,000 people take vacation motor tours in the United States each year. Nevertheless it is a mistake to regard the recent phenominal increase in automobile tourist traffic only as a source of potential hotel patronage. In his critical treatise on *Promoting New Hotels* W. I. Hamilton concludes that a majority of tourists look upon expenditures for food and lodging en route "with a cautious and conservative eye."

Not a third of the automobile tourists, except in cases of emergency or breakdown, are hotel patrons. The vast majority are patrons of the camps, the roadside cottages, and the farmhouses where the sign: "Tourists Accommodated—$1.00 per person" is the "bête noire" of the hotel keeper.[1]

Just as the coaching inns of Old England developed to meet the needs of stage-coach travelers, so the tourist camps

---

[1] P. 41.

and roadside taverns of modern times aim "to make motor trips home-like." A 1931 survey of the habitats for travelers fronting on the highway between the White House in Washington, D. C. and the capitol of Pennsylvania in Harrisburg found more than one-third as many rooms in tourist camps and homes as in hotels.[2] The new American tourist-camp industry has been recently estimated, perhaps too generously, as including "three hundred thousand shacks."[3] These small cottages serve "the need of a restless race that likes to go traveling great distances in the little old car with no great sum of money in the little old wallet."[4] In general, motor camps with individual cabins for rent become more numerous and elaborate as one travels westward and private houses with signs advertising "Rooms for Tourists" commonly serve as roadside inns near the "Tourist Meccas" of the East.

The growing popularity of these new motor inns is a disturbing factor to the managers of the second and third-rate legitimate hostelries. In their conventions and trade journals hotel men discuss methods of persuading the traveler to stay in a hotel rather than in an auto camp or tourist home. When a salesman is a regular guest, some hotels are making no extra charge for his wife. Near the cities large signs advertising various hotels flaunt such significant words as "free garage." Probably the most effective answer to tourist camp competition is the motor hotel located on the highway with separate cottages available.

In their discussion of the influence of the increasingly important automobile, Willey and Rice have made an interesting analogy between the railroad and the hotel.

---

[2] Cited by Malcolm M. Willey and Stuart A. Rice in *Communication Agencies and Social Life*, pp. 68-69.

[3] John J. McCarthy and Robert Littell, "Three Hundred Thousand Shacks," *Harpers*, CLXVII (July, 1933), 180-88.

[4] L. H. Robbins, "America Hobnobs at the Tourist Camp," *New York Times Magazine*, August 12, 1934.

At the outset of the century, both were in a strong position, and closely integrated with the habits of the people. Thirty years later, they are faced with new and "upstart" competitors which both condemn on much the same general grounds. Fundamentally, the problem involved is that of adjusting old institutions to new conditions. For railroad and hotel alike, this adjustment may come about, either by partial replacement of the older institutions in continued competition with the new, or by an integration of the new with the old.[5]

During the decade prior to the depression hotels in the United States increased both in number and in size. According to data compiled by the Engineering-Economics Foundation for a committee of hotel men, the number of better-class hotels in this country increased 29 per cent from 1920 to 1929 and the number of rooms in these hotels increased 47 per cent.[6] The number of guests, however, increased less rapidly than the number of rooms with resulting competition for patronage and improvements in service.

The trend of business in hotels has of course been markedly downward during the depression. Dr. Edward C. Romine of Horwath and Horwath made a study of the operating data for the year 1932 in 39 hotels located in 26 cities. He came to the conclusion that twenty per cent of these hotels did not earn taxes and the average hotel could not pay interest on its mortgage.[7] His firm in their monthly report on the trend of business in hotels for April 1933 announced that room sales had decreased an average of 21 per cent as compared with those of April 1932. In response to a questionnaire, sent by the author to managers of leading hotels in the larger cities of the country, one letter of explanation, dated May 25, 1933, was also received. It read in part as follows:

[5] *Op. cit.*, pp. 72-73.
[6] See charts in Hamilton, *op. cit.*, pp. 131-36.
[7] "How Many Hotels Earn Interest?"; *Hotel Monthly*, July, 1933, p. 42.

Our last winter season, owing to the depression was a dud. And our summer season promises to repeat. Our house count is running about 400 per day. Owing to our great investment we should have at least 600 per day.

The conventions, like everything else these days, have dwindled in attendance, and the delegates attending them apparently are mainly stopping out with Aunt Mary. As a result all the hotels are suffering. Last month, April, was the worst month ever experienced in local hotel business.

By April 1935, however, the average room sales, as indicated by the many well established hotels that report to Horwath and Horwath from all parts of the country, had shown a 26 per cent increase. With the coming of improved economic conditions and the growing habit of living permanently in hotels it is probable that the long-time trend in the American hotel population will be distinctly upward.

There seem to be wide variations in the travel habit between different geographic divisions, states and cities. In proportion to its population more full-time hotel guest rooms were reported by the 1930 Hotel Census for the Pacific Division than for any other section of the country, but the Atlantic Coast divisions led the others in the relative number of part-time or resort hotel guest rooms.[8] Although the cen-

---

[8] Number of Reported Guest Rooms in Hotels Having 25 or More Guest Rooms 1929 per 1,000 Population 1930.

Geographic Division	Rate for full-time hotels*	Rate for part-time hotels*
Pacific........................	24.1	0.8
Mountain......................	15.6	1.7
East North Central..............	9.8	0.6
West North Central.............	9.3	0.3
Middle Atlantic.................	9.2	2.3
West South Central.............	7.0	0.15
New England...................	6.5	4.2
South Atlantic	5.9	1.8
East South Central	3.5	0.12

* The 1930 Hotel Census covers 15,577 hotels of which 13,328 are normally

sus did not differentiate the hotel population, it did include the guest rooms mainly transient and those mainly permanent. California is the only state that has more of the latter than the former. In Pennsylvania, on the other hand, there were about one-twelfth as many rooms mainly permanent as mainly transient. San Francisco has more than three times as many hotel guest rooms as Philadelphia—almost ten times as many in proportion to its population—and more than twenty times the number of guest rooms mainly permanent. Only New York and Chicago surpass San Francisco in the number of hotel rooms.[9] If all of its 1,330 licensed

operating the entire year and 2,249 are of the resort type, operating from two to eight months of the year. Reports from 1,734 additional hotels having 25 or more guest rooms were either not received or were incomplete.

[9] Guest Rooms in Hotels Having 25 or More Guest Rooms per 1,000 Population in Cities 300,000 and Over 1930.

	Number of Rooms	Population	Rooms per 1,000 Population
Seattle	26,294	365,583	72.1
San Francisco	39,337	634,494	61.9
Portland, Oregon	14,345	301,815	47.6
Kansas City, Mo.	16,600	399,746	41.6
Minneapolis	13,817	464,356	29.7
Washington, D. C.	13,465	486,869	27.5
Chicago	83,937	3,376,438	24.8
Los Angeles	29,226	1,238,048	23.6
Indianapolis	6,805	364,161	18.7
New York	126,632	6,930,446	18.3
Detroit	27,942	1,568,662	17.8
Cincinnati	7,732	451,160	17.1
St. Louis	14,061	521,960	17.1
Boston	12,149	781,188	15.5
Cleveland	12,253	906,429	13.6
Louisville	3,866	307,745	12.6
Milwaukee	7,197	578,249	12.4
New Orleans	5,276	458,762	11.5
Buffalo	5,937	573,076	10.4
Rochester	2,958	238,132	9.0
Pittsburgh	5,901	669,817	8.8
Philadelphia	12,454	1,950,961	6.5
Newark	2,656	442,337	6.0

(Continued on next page)

hotels and lodging houses were included, rather than solely the 333 having 25 or more rooms, no city in the country—not even Seattle, using an equally inclusive definition—would show a larger relative number of hotel rooms.[10]

In contrast to the stable and conservative city of Benjamin Franklin, San Francisco is no home loving town. Most twenty-four-hour San Franciscans live in apartments or hotels and eat in restaurants. People who want their own separate houses must ride through the Twin Peaks tunnel to the neighborhoods facing the Pacific, down the peninsula toward sunny Palo Alto, across the bay to Oakland, Alameda or Berkeley, or over the Golden Gate into Marin County. With only five-eighths the percentage of children shown by the urban population as a whole, the patter of little feet on the sidewalks of San Francisco is lighter than in any other American city. Among cities over 100,000 it ranked next to Portland, Oregon, in the percentage of its population 15 years of age and over who are divorced.[11] Seattle and Los Angeles were third and fourth. San Francisco ranks first among the cities of the country in the incidence of suicide. The tradition of the mining camp and the influence of its seafaring trade seem to produce a restlessness that favors hotel life and is hostile to Puritanism.

Statistics of the hotel population, to be adequate, should

Baltimore	4,447	804,878	5.5
Jersey City	626	316,715	2.0

[10] An unpublished study of the *American Hotel Book and Supply Directory* for 1925, supplemented and checked by the *Official Hotel Red Book and Directory* for 1925, shows that San Francisco ranks first among the twenty largest cities in the United States in the number of hotel rooms it provides in proportion to its population. Seattle and Los Angeles rank second and third respectively. These three Pacific Coast cities have approximately three times as many hotel rooms for their populations as New York or Chicago. This suggests a greater mobility of population in the Far West than in the Middle West or East.

[11] See E. R. Groves and W. F. Ogburn, *American Marriage and Family Relationships* (New York, 1928), p. 439.

not only give a cross-section of this mobile group at a given time, but should also measure weekly and seasonal fluctuations and those sudden increases that come with a big convention. In the more attractive regions of the North, summer is the tourist season; in the more desirable sections of the South, on the contrary, winter is more popular. The seasonal flow of tourists, therefore, is north and south rather than east and west.

In general, weekly fluctuations are less extreme as the size of the city increases. In cities under 100,000 the percentage of occupancy during the winter is more than twice as high on Tuesday, Wednesday and Thursday as it is on Saturday and Sunday. During the summer, however, it is only one-third higher during the middle of the week. This difference can probably be accounted for by the week-end flow of vacationing metropolites to the smaller cities in the warmer months. Although the middle of the week averages four-fifths higher in cities of the 100,000 to 500,000 class, this fluctuation shows a smaller seasonal variation. In cities over 500,000 Tuesday, Wednesday and Thursday are still three-fifths higher, but there is practically no difference between summer and winter except for a Saturday drop of one-sixth during the warmer weather. In the transient hotels of New York the percentage of occupancy averages only a little more than one-fourth higher in the middle of the week.[12] The small weekly fluctuation in New York is to be explained in part by the longer average length of stay—a larger proportion remain more than a week—and by the heavier ratio of Saturday and Sunday arrivals.

That uniquely American institution, the convention, occasionally skyrockets the number of hotel guests in certain cities. According to data compiled from *World Convention Dates* the United States indulged in twice as many of these meetings in 1930 as in 1920. Although about half of the

[12] Based on Horwath and Horwath data.

7

8,501 conventions were state gatherings, the number of regional and interstate assemblies had increased during the decade almost four-fold. There seems to be a general inclination to select the larger cities for these conferences. Due, no doubt, to its central location Chicago led in the number of national and international conventions, but New York was not far behind. June, May and October, in the order named, are the most favored convention months.[13]

Distinctive patterns of sex and age distribution characterize the mobile areas of the American city. These are indicated by a study of census tracts where the population is largely housed in specific types of hotels. Such a study shows that, in contrast with the excess of children in zones of immigrant settlement or of workingmen's homes these hotel areas have a preponderance of adults. In the former most of the people are employed in the mechanical and manufacturing trades; in the latter, with the exception of the hobo area, most of the population is tied up economically with the commercial activities of the central business district. There are more than two men to each woman in the transient hotel area of Chicago; in the residential hotel area, more than three women to two men. Whereas the lodging house population is composed mostly of older homeless males, in the world of furnished rooms, not far away, the proportion of the sexes is about balanced.

A fact of special significance about these areas is the tendency for the sex and age composition to remain constant over a considerable period. Racial invasions seem to make little difference. Migration of Negroes into a rooming house area, for example, does not change its population pyramid or sex-age formation. If, however, the type of dwelling structure changes—apartments replace individual homes or tran-

---

[13] See Willey and Rice, *op. cit.*, pp. 73-77.

sient hotels deteriorate into lodging houses—the age-sex ratio invariably changes also.[14]

A study of sex and age data for census precincts in predominantly hotel, apartment and separate-house areas of Seattle gives similar results. The percentage of females rises from 12 in the district of cheap hotels to 32 in the better-class hostelries of the business center and finally to 58 in the apartment and residential hotel neighborhood. There is twice the proportion of children in the apartments as in the hotels and nine times as many in the individual homes. People who live in hotels are consistently older than apartment dwellers. The decade 35-44 leads for hotels, with 24 per cent compared with 19 in apartments; the age period 25-34 is most frequent in apartments, with 28 per cent in contrast to 22 in hotels.

EUROPEAN TOURIST MOVEMENTS

Most of the European cities and countries having reliable statistics on this subject show an increase in the hotel population up to the beginning of the depression. To cite the oldest consecutive figures available, whereas 34,700 tourists visited Copenhagen in 1864 nearly nine times that many were registered in 1929.[15] From 1911 to 1927 the number of travelers staying at hotels in Paris increased 16 per cent to a total well over two millions. During the same period hotel visitors in Berlin increased one-quarter and in Munich more than one-half.[16] Since 1906, hotels in France have decreased slightly in number, but increased in personnel.[17]

[14] See Charles Newcomb, "Graphic Presentation of Age and Sex Distribution of Population in the City" (photostated booklet, University of Chicago, 1932), pp. 91-95.   [15] *Statistisk Maanedsskrift*, 1930, p. 26.

[16] *Statistique Internationale des Grandes Villes*, pp. 274-85.

[17] A letter from the director of general statistics of France reported 35,382 hotels employing 151,672 persons for 1906 and 34,555 with a personnel of 171,938 twenty years later.

During about the same time Swiss hotels have increased both in number and in personnel.[18] In fact from the standpoint of numbers employed the hotel industry ranks second among the industries of Switzerland.

Changes in economic and political conditions quickly reflect themselves in the streams of travel. The number of tourists visiting France declined one-half between 1929 and 1932.[19] Strangers staying in the hotels and boarding houses of Budapest decreased one-fourth between 1928 and 1931.[20] A letter, dated June 16, 1934, from the director of a first-class hotel in Amsterdam outlines recent trends in the hotel business of the Dutch capital.

Before the war the better-class hotels of Amsterdam were full up from about mid-July till mid-September. For the remainder of the year they were about 75 per cent occupied, with the exception of the time of the tobacco auctions when they were mostly crowded to capacity by the leading tobacco men of the world. The post-war period up to the end of 1929 was about the same as before the war. From 1929 to the present date, however, business on the whole has been exceedingly slack owing to two causes: (1) scarcity of money among our customers and (2) the high level of the Dutch currency on account of our retaining the gold standard. The result of this is that competition among hotels is very keen. The resulting low prices, with the high overhead charges, preclude any margin of profit. In 1933 the worst months of the hotel business were in the height of the summer. There were no foreigners and local people were going more and more into the country on holidays. Only about fifty per cent of the beds were occupied during this period.

---

[18] In 1905, 5,992 hotels and boarding houses occupied a personnel of 48,953, according to the *Eidgenössisches Statistisches Amt.* By 1929 the corresponding figures were 7,772 hotels and 63,258 persons.

[19] See Marcel Gautier, "Les Industries Touristiques et L'Hotellerie," *Revue D'Economie Politique*, 1933, p. 1005.

[20] Based on a letter from Dr. L. I. Illyefalvi, director of the Municipal Statistics Bureau of Budapest.

During the summer of 1933 when the better-class hotels of Amsterdam had so few patrons, the United Kingdom experienced a four per cent increase in foreign visitors over the preceding summer. Tourists from countries like France, Germany and Holland, for whom the rate of exchange was favorable, showed marked increases. An editorial in the *London Times* for November 4, 1933 urged trade people against "over-charging or discourtesy or insular impatience" in serving these Continental visitors.

Professor F. W. Ogilvie in his critical economic study of *The Tourist Movement* concludes that "all the world over the same broad features are visible: an increase in the number of tourists up to 1929-30 and a diminution thereafter, the fluctuations being in close sympathy with fluctuations in general business; and, irrespective of fluctuations, an increased 'vulgarization' of the traffic according to class of travel, with diminished expenditure in any one place or country."[21] This "vulgarization" may be seen in the decline since the war of first, cabin and second-class steamship passengers and the increase of tourist and third-class travelers.[22] Between 1923 and 1930 first-class railway travel to Italy by foreigners declined from 28 to 11 per cent and third-class increased from 29 to 53 per cent. Although the number of foreign visitors to Italy increased more than two-fifths during this period the average length of stay decreased almost one-third and the total expenditure decreased about one-sixth.[23]

The people in some countries like to travel; those in others prefer to act as hosts. The United States, the United King-

---

[21] P. 140. On p. 4 Professor Ogilvie differentiates between migrants who "change their residence for a year or more" and tourists "who stay away from home for any period not exceeding one year."

[22] Gautier, *op. cit.*, p. 1006.

[23] Ogilvie, *op. cit.*, pp. 162 and 157.

dom, the Dutch East Indies, Germany, the Union of South Africa, Argentina and Sweden, in the order named, rank on the debit side of international tourist balances; France, Canada, Italy, Switzerland and Austria, on the credit side. American tourists abroad spent about one-third more than the combined tourists from all the other twenty-three countries reporting to the League of Nations.[24] In 1931 Americans spent more money in France than in the rest of Europe put together, but more in Canada than in Europe.[25]

European tourist movements are rather heavily concentrated in the summer months. Norway finds that 75 per cent of her foreign tourists arrive in June, July and August. The United Kingdom receives about 40 per cent of its foreign visitors in July, August and September; Yugo-Slavia, 43 per cent in the same period.[26] With interesting local exceptions, the tourist traffic from outside is also highest in Germany, Switzerland, Austria and Czechoslovakia during these months. Italy, however, has two seasons—one with a peak in April and the other reaching its greatest height in August or September.

The man who tells in the interview below about fluctuations in the hotel population of Munich and Florence was born in the hotel his father owned in Strassburg, the business center for Alsace. When the war was over and Alsace became a part of France his father was ordered to move out with one hundred pounds of baggage for each member of the party. Eventually he was reimbursed for one-third the

<hr />

[24] *Balances of Payments 1930* (Geneva, 1932), pp. 41-43.

[25] Ogilvie, *op. cit.*, p. 218. Although the amount declined 17 per cent between 1929 and 1932, tourist expenditure in Canada for 1932—with the expenditure of Canadian tourists in other countries deducted—was of greater value than any single commodity exported in the same year. See *The Canada Year Book 1933*, p. 598.

[26] Ogilvie, *op. cit.*, pp. 83, 170 and 182. Although European statistics of tourism ordinarily show these seasonal variations, with the exception of those for the United Kingdom and Copenhagen, they do not distinguish between men and women.

value of his property in Alsace. The son, Herr Direktor von Strassburg, has served two years each in American and Florentine hotels. He is now director of one of the leading hostelries of Munich.

The passion play at Oberammergau every tenth year (1920, 1930) causes an unusually high point in tourist traffic to Munich. The years preceding and following this play tend to be poor; 1924 to 1928 were normal.

July, August and September make up the season. The English come to Munich in August—not always the nicest class. There is also considerable movement in January and February—many carnivals and fancy-dress balls. July and August are the best months for Americans, most of whom come from New York City or Chicago.

Berlin is the principal source for German trade; the industrial areas of the Rhone and Ruhr valleys come next. Stuttgart is the most important source for Bavarian patronage. The October Fest draws from the country villages; this celebration is the best place to see the care-free character of the Bavarian peasant. The week-end is quiet in Munich because many people make *Ausfluge* or expeditions to nearby lakes and mountains.

To the German a hotel is a place to stay overnight. If a state official comes here from Berlin he may stay a week, or even a month, but he moves to a house as soon as possible. The apartment hotel is unknown in Munich and unwanted. We do not like to live in hotels like Americans.

The season for individual tours in Florence is March, April and May with the peak in April. For conducted parties, ranging in size from 40 to 250, July and August is the season. The conducted tour business was built up after the war and has fallen with the crisis. Italy is the only major country in Europe where the de luxe hotel is not visited by natives. Out of 225 guests in my hotel only 2 would be Italians.

Guests do not stay as long as formerly. The multiplication of transportation connections, the increasing use of automobiles and the growing importance of the airplane are factors that make stays shorter. People rush through life and through countries. Tourists must do Italy in a week. They see more, perhaps, but not as fundamentally.

There is a story that shows the new type of tourist. A daughter said to her mother, "We must go to Florence." "But we have already been there, my dear." "No, we haven't, mother." "Why, yes, we have. That's the place where we bought the silk shawl."

A wealthy American matron had just motored from Rome through the hill towns to Florence. Arriving at the hotel she raved about how beautiful they were. Then a lady asked her, "What were the names of some of these towns?" "John," she said, turning to her chauffeur, "could you tell the lady what the names of the towns were?"

CHAPTER VII

TYPES OF HOTEL DWELLERS

In this modern day of cheap and rapid transportation almost every American has had some contact with hotels. Workers and business men, teachers and debutantes, actors and salesmen, people who are distinguished and many who would like to be, governors and gamblers, opera singers and hobos—all these have their favorite hotels.

The large metropolitan hostelry houses a cosmopolitan assemblage. In the lobby throng one might find a Main Street banker rubbing elbows unknowingly with a professional crook, or a retired farmer on a trip to the city jostling a theatrical "headliner." Here also are society women, buyers for department stores, bachelors, an occasional family, women of disrepute, "four flushers" and men of affairs. Business men and their wives frequently run in to the metropolis from villages in the hinterland to do a little business and shopping and to "take in" the latest offerings of the city's theatres. "Recently two young women stopped at the hotel who were obviously from a small town," said a room clerk. "At about seven-thirty they came up to the desk and announced that they were going to a movie and might be back late. Would I please tell them when the doors were closed as they did not want to be locked out."

In the hotel lobby are also the round-the-world travelers who have come in contact, for the most part, with various kinds of cosmopolitanism. They usually stop in the cities; only rarely are the rural sections visited. In the city they stay at a more or less Grand Hotel; not in a private home with its distinctive culture. Experiences in these hotels frequently color the traveler's impression of an entire country. An American in Australia was heard to remark: "What good is this country anyway—not even running ice-water in the hotel."

Occasionally hotels may come to be considered as ends in themselves. When the traveler tells about his European tour, supposedly made for an artistic or educational purpose, he may inadvertently advise: "Don't miss Dinkelsbühl when you are motoring through Bavaria. There is such a good hotel there!"

The cosmopolitan hotel population is also interesting historically. During the seventeenth and eighteenth centuries prince and pauper, soldier and pilgrim, horses and men were all entertained at the roadside inn. With the development of railway travel three new groups became noticeably important: first, salesmen; second, actors; and third, women.

The bagman, a forerunner of the first group, had appeared in England by the latter part of the eighteenth century. "Not a term of approbrium, this, by any means. Think of the immediate forerunner of the present-day commercial traveler, sitting astride a sturdy horse with a well-stocked bag on each side, facing all weathers, negotiating all roads, and making a journey of a month or two at a time."[1] The bagman probably appeared in America before 1830. After the Civil War he gradually substituted sample-grips and trunks for carpetbags, and, since his job was to drum up business for his company, he became known as a "drummer." In 1883 his numbers were estimated by the *Hotel Gazette* at more than two hundred thousand.[2] He provided a large proportion of the transient trade in urban commercial houses and practically all the patronage in small cities and towns.

[1] Maskell and Gregory, *op. cit.*, pp. 210-12.

[2] Williamson, *op. cit.*, pp. 123-25.

Although in recent years hotels in the smaller centers supplement their income from the seasonal flow of automobile tourists, they are still largely supported by traveling salesmen. As an example, a commercial hotel in La Crosse, Wisconsin, a city of about forty thousand inhabitants, caters almost exclusively to the traveling man. The telephone operator in this hotel describes these modern bagmen as follows :

Traveling salesmen make up the bulk of our guests. Their wares vary from silk hose to candy, automobile accessories, meat and Delco lights. Probably the automobile accessories salesmen are the most numerous. The men are usually young, some starting out on their first trips. They often form their closest friendships with those selling the same article—there were three tire men who were inseparable—but this is not always the case. I remember three men whom we called the "Triumvirate." One was a salesman for safes and deposit boxes ; another was an agent for a Chicago brand of men's clothing ; and the third was a lumber man. Although many of these men have friends in town whom they visit evenings and Sundays, as a general rule they try to get acquainted with the permanent guests and with the management so as to feel somewhat more at home on their next visit. Of all the guests, this group is the easiest to please and the least bothersome.

With the rise of the chain store system of marketing and the decreasing need for traveling representatives the number of salesmen is said to have declined to a point less than half that in 1910. The automobile seems to have had the effect of eliminating salesmen from the guests at the village inn. Establishing headquarters in a larger town, the present-day commercial traveler can drive out to his customers in the smaller places of the hinterland and return to his hotel or even to his permanent home at night. Although in the past men of the road have had a divorce rate more than double the average for all occupations, the modern salesman has the possibility, under this new arrangement, of a more stable home life.

Distinctive personality traits have long been attributed to the traveling man. "The bagman of old was a picturesque individual," wrote Jefferson Williamson. "He was a gay dog personally, a heartbreaker among the ladies, with a lass in every port, and an industrious conveyor of smutty stories throughout the length and breadth of the land." If the twentieth century salesman has lost some of his original wildness, he still retains sufficiently distinctive occupational peculiarities to enable clever front-office employees to identify him. "I can tell a salesman the minute he comes to the counter," said Harry J. Rottman, at that time clerk of the Congress Hotel in Chicago. "In fact, I can generally spot him clear across the lobby."

He walks as if he knew just where he was going and what he meant to do when he got there. At the counter he turns the book around for himself without waiting for the clerk to do it for him, helps himself to a pen, dashes off his name, and puts the pen back where it belongs. He doesn't ask what kind of a room he can get—he tells you what kind he wants. He knows all the ropes —and he likes to show that he knows them. If he's acquainted with the clerk, even only slightly, he calls him by his first name; and he likes to be called by his first name. He talks fast, likes to chaff and to be chaffed, and likes to impress bystanders with the fact that he is an insider.[3]

European hotel men also recognize the salesman as a distinct type. Some of them cater to him; others do not. The Herr Direktor von Wien, quoted in chapter III, differentiated clearly between the salesman and the intellectual.

The traveling salesman does not like this hotel. To him it is a dead hole—a cemetery. He wants a hotel where there is life.

---

[3] Allison Gray, "How the Hotel Clerk Sizes You Up," *The American Magazine*, XCIV (November, 1922), 54-55.

Life means business. He wants a restaurant with a long menu and three waiters—a head waiter, a regular waiter and a wine boy. He wants to be near the theatres and see the pretty dancing girls.

The intellectual is quite different in his tastes. He is disturbed by traffic at night and enjoys a quiet hotel like this. He does not care for a big menu—does not know whether it is cauliflower or potato he is eating. Perhaps a choice between beefsteak and chicken. That is all. Only one waiter is necessary and he should make the decisions for him. He wants to be free to think. In walking to the hotel he chooses a quiet street. He has an idea in his mind and might lose it if there are many people to jostle. The salesman, on the other hand, likes the busy street. He might meet some beautiful girls.

During the eighties and the gay nineties, before the movies, the automobile and the radio had killed many of them off, theatrical troupers supplied an important share of the trade in a large number of hotels. Although numerically less important then the salesman, the actor was even more colorful. The stage had not yet become respectable and "touring actors still retained a joyous and gypsy irregularity."[4] Divorce statistics for 1906 give actors the winning rate —seven times the average for all occupations. Their mobility, their Bohemian moral code and their intimate contacts with the members of the opposite sex were no doubt factors.

Even at the present time practically every city of any size—say 100,000—has at least one actor's hotel that caters definitely to theatrical people. This is usually one of the older and less desirable hostelries. Only "headliners" can go to the Grand Hotel. To the hotel man the actor is one of the most difficult and distressing types of guests. When business is good, his patronage is not encouraged. Pet dogs, monkeys and even lizzards are frequently combined with a small income and an erratic temperament. A well known actress,

---

[4] Lewis, *op. cit.*, p. 133.

who moved audiences to tears with her acting, was not long ago forced to leave an ultra-fashionable hotel in Chicago because of the untidy way she kept her room, her custom of giving parties after the play, making demands on the maids at five o'clock in the morning, sleeping in the daytime instead of at night, and temperamental behavior in general.

The telephone operator, quoted above, also wrote about theatrical people.

Actors usually arrive early in the morning and insist on lower rates. They can be distinguished at once by their extreme and flashy clothes, their slouchy walk and their incorrect grammar. They usually make themselves very much at home, allowing their children absolute freedom which is often disgusting and pitiful. But there is another type among theatrical people. They are more cultured and refined. It is interesting to see these actors off stage and to find that they are very much like us.

Before the Civil War some married women lived permanently in hotels or traveled with their husbands, but respectable hostelries would not give shelter at night to unaccompanied ladies. Much later in the nineteenth century a woman would not think of using the main entrance of a hotel. She always went in at the ladies' entrance. Since old registers frequently contained comments too virile for feminine reading, she did not sign the register in person. Even today the stigma attached to hotel life for young women tends to persist in the smaller cities of the East. Just a few years ago a school teacher in Salem, Massachusetts, declined to eat dinner with a gentleman friend in the best hotel of that city. She might be fired from her position!

Miss Pennington, a Seattle school teacher, has lived in hotels practically all of the time since 1908. Because her teaching has taken her to different parts of the country she has been a permanent guest in both the East and the West. Her first experience was at the outstanding hotel in Spokane. At first the free and easy life surprised and shocked her, but soon she enjoyed the ease of making acquaintances and the numerous social contacts. Included among the guests was a high percentage of transient men and in company with her roommate, another teacher, Miss Pennington had an exceptionally good time.

The difference in attitude toward women who live in hotels was keenly felt in the next town where she taught. Remembering the pleasant social life of her previous experience she planned to live in a hotel with another schoolma'am. The customs of this town in New York State were very conventional and fixed, however. It was considered improper for single women to live in hotels so they were forced to stay at the more "respectable" boarding house.

In 1885 only 11 per cent of the guests at New York's four largest hotels were women. Of all the people entertained during the year 1926 by one of the foremost hotels of that city 37 per cent were women. In the better-class transient hotels of the United States as a whole about 30 per cent of the population are women. According to the 1933 survey of leading hotels in 11 cities, cited in chapter VI, the average percentage of women among *permanent* guests was 41. A special study of sixteen Seattle hotels having a minimum rate of one dollar or more showed 43 per cent of the population female. More than two-thirds of these Seattle women were living alone.

While recent social changes have decreased the numbers of salesmen and actors, one of these trends—the phenomenal rise of the automobile—has stimulated travel by women. In many of the larger cities there are now hotels, like the Martha Washington in New York, which cater exclusively to women. Generally speaking, however, women as well as men prefer the co-educational institution.

It is common knowledge among managers that women are more critical than men. Hotel men agree that the increasing number of the more discriminating sex has had an

important influence on furnishings and service. How to meet
the demands of this new public is a favorite topic for hotel
conventions and trade journals.

A man at a hotel alone does not behave like a man who is
accompanied by his wife. The one with his wife along appears
to be more complaining and more difficult to please. This is
largely because the wife being in the hotel more than her husband in the course of the day, and knowing more about the de-
tails of good housekeeping, may notice things that would escape
her husband's attention. Then she tells him about them—perhaps in an if-you're-a-real-man-you'll-have-this-remedied tone—
and he feels duty bound to go to the desk and enlighten the clerk
about the inferiority of the service. Furthermore, a woman is
often more insistent than a man on getting her money's worth.[5]

It was pointed out above that in the residential hotel
areas of Chicago there are more than three women for every
two men. A study of eight residential hotels in Seattle and
Tacoma shows practically the same ratio. Since there was
a much greater preponderance of males in the hotel population of the past, this growing number of the other sex may
be thought of as an aspect of the general movement among
women against slavish drudgery and towards a freedom that
will permit self-expression. There are now many traveling
salesladies who use hotels like their masculine prototype.
There are also women buyers for big department stores,
private secretaries, physicians, business executives, and teachers who prefer to live in hotels where they can have more
freedom and comfort than in private homes or apartments.
A distinguished literary person can be as isolated in her
hotel room as in a cabin in the north woods and yet meet
and talk with people at will. Relieved from household cares
and responsibilities, she can devote all her time and energy

---

[5] Fred C. Kelly, "Human Nature in the Lobby," *Hotel Management*, May,
1922.

to the production of literature. As indicated in the introduction, however, not all women in hotels use their time so constructively. Many of them have gained their freedom but lost their direction.

CHAPTER VIII

EMANCIPATED FAMILIES

THE HOMESTEAD of the American pioneer was the focus for a large, integrated, semi-patriarchal family in which the wishes of the individual were usually sacrificed to the interests of the group. When a man married he sought more than a companion; he wanted a business partner. Children were regarded with affection, to be sure, but they were also valued for the work they could do. The individual in the small, loosely integrated family of the present day has largely broken away from subservience to the wishes of his relatives. The many functions performed by the colonial family have markedly declined and affection is the most important remaining bond that holds the group together. Especially in the larger cities is there a trend toward multiple dwellings, life without property, numerous activities outside of the home and the farming out of babies as in Moscow.

How many of us realize how modern a phenomenon is the small family of father, mother and children emancipated from the control of the wider kinship group of grandparents, uncles, aunts and cousins? Do we perceive that it is to be found as a typical specimen perhaps only in cities, and particularly in urbanized areas of our very largest American cities? The small family group in apartment houses and residential hotels is, no doubt, the most notorious illustration of effectual detachment from the claims of kinship. The absence in the city home of the "spare bedroom," that famous institution of the country-side, serves as a convenient defense against invading relatives.[1]

---

[1] Ernest W. Burgess, "The Family as a Unity of Interacting Personalities," *The Family*, March, 1926.

The smaller the family the greater the likelihood that it will live in a hotel. When the Chicago families studied by Day Monroe consisted of husband and wife alone there was six times the likelihood of lodging, i.e. living in rooming houses or hotels, as when there were three in the group and twenty-four times as compared with the family of four.[2] From the student survey of Seattle hotels, described in chapter III, it was found that in the 220 hostelries for which the schedules seemed to be complete and accurate there were more than two and one-half times as many couples without children as couples with children.[3] Although these facts indicate that the hotel is, generally speaking, a natural habitat for childless families, different types of hotels vary in the extent to which this is true. In the better-class transient hotels of the United States one-fifth of the registrations are for man and wife; in resort hotels, one-third;[4] in apartment hotels, probably more than three-fifths.

Rather than skimp along on one meagre income, many

---

[2] Day Monroe, *Chicago Families: a Study of Unpublished Census Data*, pp. 74-75.

[3] Composition of the Hotel Population in Seattle:

Class	Number	Percentage
Total house count......................	10,961	100
Males..................................	7,854	71.7
Females................................	3,107	28.3
Couples with children....................	226	......
Couples without children.................	594	10.8
	(1,188 individuals)	
Lone* males	7,000	63.9
Lone* females..........................	2,156	19.8
Guests over 60.........................	784	7.2
Children under 12......................	203	1.9

* This means living alone. In most cases these guests are also single, i.e. unmarried.

[4] According to data from Horwath and Horwath 90 transient hotels average 23 per cent of the registrations two in a room and 16 resort hotels average 39 per cent. Probably 90 per cent of the two-in-a-room registrations are for man and wife.

young couples prefer to work for two salaries and live in a
hotel free from household responsibilities. They like the
prestige such an abode gives them, for it means more socially to say that one lives at the Fairmont, if it is San Francisco, than at 813 Clay Street. Then, too, they may have
been accustomed to a high standard of dress and dwelling
and hesitate to lower it when married. In the hotel they are
not only emancipated from the control of the kinship group,
but also from the obligations of neighborhood life and from
the care of children. True, sometimes children arrive un-
invited making the families "orthodox." Under these circumstances they usually move to apartments or bungalows.
More commonly, however, conscious family limitation is
successful and, although the couples may dream about the
little cottage or the grandiose mansion, they sometimes find
old age upon them and are still unable to quit the life to
which they have become adjusted.

While in Chicago, Mr. and Mrs. Walters lived in an apartment
house in the Wilson Avenue district, not far from Sheridan Road.
Mrs. Walters had watched with interest the arrivals and depart-
ures of the young couple who lived in the apartment just above
them. The woman was always beautifully clothed, with something new nearly every time she was observed. The man was a
broker. Mrs. Walters decided that she was very clearly not in
the same class with them. But she was "oh, so lonesome" and
she didn't know anyone with whom to talk.

Then one day there was a commotion in the hall outside her
door. She investigated. There she found the big Russian wolf
hound belonging to the couple above, in the throes of a paralytic
stroke with his mistress standing by much agitated.

Together the two women carried the sick dog to the floor
above. Since they proved to be equally lonesome, this singular
incident was the beginning of a close friendship. And now, although they live in widely separated cities and several years
have elapsed, they still correspond.

Besides the Chicago experience, in the four years since their

marriage Mrs. Walters and her husband have lived in hotels or
small apartments in several towns not far away. Mr. Walters
spends four or five months in each city establishing a branch
sales department for electrical appliances. He then places a
salesman in charge and moves to another center. Eventually
they plan to live permanently in Chicago.

Mrs. Walters has an elaborate assortment of embroideries.
When she tires of amusing herself with the radio in her hotel
room she takes her fancy work to the lobby just for the sense of
nearness to human beings.[5]

This mobile childless family is detached from the local
community and does not participate in its activities other
than to meet the demands of business. At first the wife accompanied her husband as a lonesome woman of leisure
who must take her fancy work into the lobby "just for the
sense of nearness to human beings." In some cities she partially overcame this lonesomeness by working as a telephone
operator. The unique episode of the Russian wolf hound
suggests dramatically the extent of seclusion in the apartment
and hotel areas of great cities. If this dog had not had a
paralytic stroke at her apartment door Mrs. Walters would
probably have remained better acquainted with St. Paul
than with the woman who lived just above her.

There are also many elderly couples, particularly in residential hotels. Sometimes an institution of this kind comes
to have so many guests of mature years that it is nicknamed
"The Old People's Home." With their children married
these elderly people have retired from their customary duties
and responsibilities. Many men and women, who have
worked hard in their younger years and saved a little money,
enjoy living in comfort and ease for the remainder of their
days. In a hotel they have an opportunity to do many things
that in the press of more important affairs have been left
undone. Here they may be independent and live their own

---

[5] An interview by Una Middleton Hayner.

lives in any way they see fit. They too are emancipated.

The study of Chicago families, cited above, showed more than five times the tendency to live in rooming houses or hotels among families of professional men as compared with those of unskilled laborers. "The three groups in which the percentage of families lodging was highest were the professional, executive, and salaried classes, where social conventions lead to the greatest likelihood of democratic family organization."[6] In these groups the wife plays an important rôle in family discussions, has many interests outside of the home and likes to delegate the care of her children to nursemaids and private schools. If there are no children she may urge moving to a hotel to escape the responsibilities of maintaining her own home. In the "paternal family" of the laborer the husband, who is the dominant member of the group, is usually neither able nor willing to free his wife from her household duties.

Women of Leisure

There is some tendency for housewifely habits to persist after a woman moves to a hotel. Even when the facilities are not provided there are many guests in residential hostelries who do a little cooking in their rooms. Electrical appliances of various kinds and alcohol lamps are used for this purpose. There is a family of four who live permanently in one large room of a commercial hotel. The mother cooks meals on two small grills and her electric iron. They frequently have a guest for dinner! But this is an exceptional case. Light breakfasts cooked in the room or tea for a friend seem to be most popular. All manner of devices from waste baskets to prevarications attempt to conceal these undertakings from the management.

These methods of concealment are not always successful.

---

[6] Monroe, *op. cit.*, p. 66.

It is reported that a bottle of milk, knocked accidentally from the window where a well-to-do family was living, fell three stories to the street and just missed hitting the hotel manager's head! A woman called up the office during an interview, said she was sick in bed and objected to the "horrible" smells of food cooking. She herself was known to be one of the worst offenders along this line! A package that had fallen from an eleventh floor window, was picked up by the gardener and found to contain beefsteak. The odor of cooking onions has been detected in the hallways of a fashionable hotel. A resident in a house, which also provides no culinary arrangements in its rooms, created a scandal by buying meat at the corner market. She was in the habit of cooking lunch for her little girl who was attending school.

All of these doings we concealed from the employees, locking dishes and food in a trunk which is kept solely for that purpose. We close the door with the extra lock which no one except the hotel manager is supposed to be able to open. When this lock is on, the maid is not to disturb us unless we have given her other orders. I paid seven cents a pint for milk at a nearby grocer's and twenty-five for a like amount, from the same dairy, at the hotel. Eggs and fruit cost one-half to one-third outside. It is sometimes rather a problem to appear in the lobby looking quite innocent when I have in my arms a pint of milk, a half pint of cream, fruit, and a half dozen eggs. Because of this I do not always ask for my mail.

This persistent effort to cook in the rooms was undoubtedly one reason for the increasing number of apartment hotels with kitchenettes. In these hotels, however, the restaurant and room service seem to have proved more popular than was at first anticipated.

We have found that people are having an increasingly large number of meals served in their rooms, meals cooked in our kitchens and delivered in the apartment ready to serve. Neither our restaurants nor our kitchen space were planned quite large enough, a result probably of the fact that when this was done, we still had a lot to learn about human nature as exemplified by people when living in an apartment of this sort. The kitchenettes are used more for the preparation of breakfast, tea or for a late evening supper than at other times in the day. These facts, I feel, point to the trend of things.[7]

But the active housewife who cooks meals and cares for children is the exception in the hotel home. Unemployed wives of "cliff dwellers" are more likely to be interested in dress and "society" than in anything else. The large place given to articles of apparel in the ground floor shops that are to be found in many hotels is suggestive of the fashion and front by which one is judged in the public rooms. On the street floor of one of these great institutions the largest space is taken by a permanent wave specialist. There are also a photographer's studio, a shop for wool where knitting is taught, a gown and hat store and a shop specializing in "attire for the larger woman." On the main floor of this hotel is a shop offering fancy cushions and all kinds of lamps, little else. The hotel druggist says that his greatest sale in number of articles is for rouge and similar cosmetics, while the largest business in dollars is for perfumes.

Although the percentage of employed women seems to vary in different sections of the country and in different classes of hotels, it is usually small in temporary domiciles of the better type. The manager of a large hotel home in Chicago estimated that less than 10 per cent of his women patrons were employed for a monetary return. In another residential hotel, which caters to a rather wealthy class in the same city, only about 2 per cent of the women had any remunerative employment.

"Hotel life is all right for elderly people," said the manager

---

[7] Adapted from Wilbur T. Emerson, "Managing Apartment Hotels," *Hotel Management*, March, 1924. Mr. Emerson was vice-president and managing director of the Hotels Windermere in Chicago when he wrote the article.

of a large family hotel, "but it makes bums out of women." This applies particularly to young married women with nothing to do. They spend their time shopping, attending social functions, playing bridge. They rise rather late, smoke a good deal and become "absolutely useless."

I was more alert in my own home. As there is no housework in the hotel I lead a rather indolent life. I walk about aimlessly, find it difficult to get exercise, overeat and become overfat.[8]

"You are so busy, Miss Lee," said the chambermaid one day. Although she was typing at the moment, the lady addressed had really found it difficult to keep busy and was surprised at the remark. The maid then told her that other women lay in bed until noon or even two o'clock, reading novels and perhaps munching chocolates. "Sun dodgers" she called them.

Another maid in the same hotel thought that at least half of the women there were very lazy and led quite useless lives. This type, she said, would have breakfast at noon or later, would do a little in the room, or, not so often, go out and play cards. Then she would have a beauty nap, always a beauty nap, and very often would go downstairs to have her nails manicured and her hair dressed. Miss Lee remarked that she had never had this done. "Oh," the maid laughed, "if you don't have your nails and hair done almost every day, you are not a lady." Then there would be baths and mud baths. After that she would dress for dinner and do something in the evening, either in the hotel or outside.

This maid thought that people in the hotel did not want to bother with children. Married couples drifted apart easily because there was little to hold them. The wife had nothing to do and perhaps fell in love with another man. If her husband was away much, she was particularly apt to become

---

[8] Interview with a married woman who has had a long experience in hotels both in this country and in Europe.

interested in someone else. Once the maid was in the room when a quarrel was going on and heard the husband say, "I have been working hard all day and you have been doing nothing. Couldn't you at least do a little washing of a few things, in your room?" "Oh, I can easily get someone else to support me if you don't want to," the lady replied.

I have noticed that man and wife in a hotel find a lot to quarrel about. They frequently have a hot time in the middle of the night which ends when one of them goes downstairs and rents another room until morning.[9]

Hotel life seems to facilitate family disorganization. There is no common life to hold the group together. Members easily become individualized and readily develop divergent attitudes. If "response" or affection fails, no other bond remains. The Wilson Avenue district in Chicago, for example, has a larger number of better-class residential hotels than any other community in the city; it also has the highest rate for family disintegration.[10] In fact, the relative number of both hotel rooms and divorces increases as one moves westward from the Atlantic through the Central to the Western states.

The hotel environment no doubt accentuates those tensions that are the real causes of domestic discord. It also provides a refuge for the divorced. Here are men and women who are trying to overcome the disillusionment of an unhappy marriage. "Effie," a character created by Sinclair Lewis, "met a whole society of detached women dwelling in hotels, idle women, mostly living on alimony and displaying energy only when they dragged their husbands into court."[11]

In spite of the difficulties incident to maintaining a home

---

[9] Adapted from a paper by the daughter of a hotelkeeper.
[10] See Ernest R. Mowrer, *Family Disorganization* (Chicago, 1927), pp. 116-19.
[11] *Op. cit.*, pp. 291-92.

under the conditions of modern city life and the attractions of the hotel—its freedom, its comfort, its relative cheapness —it frequently takes a crisis, such as desertion or divorce, to break up the habits that bind the individual or family to a particular place. Sickness or a "nervous breakdown" may make housekeeping impossible. The landlord may double the rent. The departure of son and daughter from home may encourage the move. In many cases death itself is the immediate cause. Two sisters, whose stay in the hotel was to have been only temporary, "do not have the heart to return to their large suburban home because of the mother's sudden death. There are many such "tag ends" or fragments of families in hotels. In fact the hotel family is more frequently the beginning or ending of an association rather than the fully rounded normal group.

The greatest crisis of my life forced this change upon me. This crisis was the breaking up of an exceptionally happy home through the death within a period of about two years, of four of my nearest relatives—my sister, my brother and his two sons. For eight years my home had been with my sister on my brother's 250,000 acre ranch high in the New Mexico Rockies. The transition from that luxurious home and the free life of those glorious mountains to the restricted existence of a room in a city hotel was a bitter experience, and the contrast in the two modes of life threw into high relief the deficiencies of hotels and the annoyance of the proximity of too many neighbors. Life, even in hotels like the Blackstone in Chicago or The Palace in San Francisco—in both of which I have stayed—or in high priced resort hotels here and abroad, has never, in my opinion, compared with the refreshing comfort of the home of a well-to-do family. The most extravagant hotel menu cannot vie with a carefully supervised home table.[12]

A tendency toward portliness in women of leisure does

---

[12] By the woman who had lived for brief periods in about five hundred hotels. See p. 1.

not appear to be limited to any particular creed or nation-ality. It seems to be natural for both Jew and Gentile under the conditions of hotel life. The following conversation took place between a waiter and a guest in an Irish-Catholic hotel home.

"You do not wish bread tonight, madam?"

"Not bread and potato, too. That makes one fat."

"Ha, ha. The ladies are all afraid to get fat."

"And the men? Are not they also afraid?"

"Oh, no. The men, they work hard. They do not get fat. But the ladies! They sit and play cards; they sit and talk. All the time they just do this and so they get fat."

There is one form of indulgence which all Jewish people seem to permit themselves and that is food. There is always good food and plenty of it even in the home of the poor immigrant. But these poor people don't get fat; they work too hard. When the Jew gets rich, however, he starts to take on weight. The man usually keeps his shape until after he retires. But the young girls get fat soon after they get married. They have no work to do. They stay in bed until late in the morning, take life easy and eat a lot of very expensive and fattening food. They seem to be con-cerned about their weight; they are always trying to get thin; but they do not seem to care enough about it to give up the food they like. It is a common joke among Jewish people who smile knowingly when one of their number insists that she is dieting and·"just can't get thin."[13]

As pointed out in chapter I, the men who patronize the better-class hotels are to a large extent men of affairs.[14] They regard the hotel as a convenience, a thing to be used.

In the morning the women would meet and plan their day or discuss what had happened "last night at the dance." In the evening these same women would meet for just a minute before going calling, playing bridge, or, if there were any busy mothers

[13] From a paper on "The Jewish Hotel," by a patron.
[14] P. 8.

among them, going to their rooms to "darn the children's stockings." One would seldom find men present in the lobby after dinner, for they preferred the pool room, going there to smoke and talk over the latest financial and political news. Many a woman bemoaned the loss of a perfectly good husband when she moved to the hotel, but really when one stops to think about it, it did offer a very easy meeting place for men of affairs. And there were busy and important men living there too, men who were identified with large corporations, men who managed railroads and other such enterprises.

The lazy indolent society woman contrasted vividly with the busy man of affairs. Her chief occupation consisted in frittering away the day in an unprofitable manner, playing bridge, dabbling at this and that, fussing about her clothes, her looks, and the bored life she led.[15]

Interest in comfort and food appear to dominate in the following impressionistic description, by a fellow hotel dweller, of a "social leader" in a residential hotel. The conversation suggests a certain emptiness frequently found in people of this type.

Today I went downtown in the coach with a lady who is said to be one of the leaders in the permanent set. There were four persons in the coach. Mrs. Beach evidently knew well the other two, a man and his wife, and carried on a stream of conversation with the man during the half-hour journey. The wife spoke only three times. Mrs. Beach is rather tall and stout, in her early fifties, I should say. Her face is plump, pretty, quite expressionless and considerably made up—the usual amount of rouge. She carefully picked out the most comfortable, protected corner of the coach and proceeded to talk in a soft, measured, comfortable tone which somehow suggested that she was at the same time enjoying a whipped cream puff.

The man, I gathered, had been quite ill with the same sickness that Mr. Beach had suffered, so the conversation ran entirely on that subject and on food which the two men might safely eat.

---

[15] "Two Years in a Residential Hotel."

The chief line advanced by Mrs. Beach was that she had food specially prepared by the Maitre d'hotel himself. All other ways had failed. "He is an Italian, you know, and has been all over the world. We have met him in Paris and London. He can cook anything as well as you could get it anywhere. I pay him liberally. I go to him in the morning and ask what special dish can be had today, and if that does not do I order anything I think best. For instance, he will take a large chicken and make the most delicious chicken soup. He makes an Italian rice pudding sort of thing which is perfectly wonderful."

An official in the Women's City Club in Chicago, who did society reporting for a year, is of the opinion that the majority of people living in "high-class residential hotels are motivated by a liking for ease and ostentation. People can make more show of expensive living and entertaining at a hotel for less money and trouble than in their own homes. She was amazed at the cheap luncheons women would give —seventy-five cents per plate or even fifty cents, amounting to no more than afternoon tea—followed by an announcement in the newspaper that "Mrs. So-and-so entertained fifty guests at luncheon in the Plaza Hotel, the company afterwards playing bridge."

Society women are often more interested in club meetings and social functions than in their children, if they have any. One hotel employs a trained kindergartner to care for the fifty or sixty children that live there in the summer time. Between twelve and two in the afternoon these children are released, ostensibly for a little family life with their mothers, but the latter are frequently too busy with other matters to pay any attention to them.

An individual's conception of his rôle in modern industrial society, according to Thorstein Veblen, is determined by the self-conscious attitudes of "invidious comparison" and "conspicuous expenditure." "Non-productive consumption of time," reinforced by these attitudes, gives the individual a higher status in society and satisfies his wish for recognition. "The dress of women goes even farther than that of men in the way of demonstrating the wearer's abstinence from productive employment."[16] This theory helps to explain the extreme and ostentatious peacock dressing, sometimes quite daring or even startling in design, which is displayed by women of wealth and leisure in the luxurious dining rooms of our most fashionable caravanseries.

Hartley Withers makes clear in the following statement the choice open to members of the leisure class, a choice as to what they shall do with their time.

A leisure class that uses its leisure to do public work that is otherwise done ill or left undone is certainly a national asset, but it cannot be denied that under the capitalistic system there has existed a class of most unamiable folk who lived narrow, selfish lives on wealth that they had inherited, grumbled at paying taxes, forgetting that if the Government did not protect them and their property they would be quite unable to earn a living, and seemed to expect the whole world to be managed for their convenience and comfort. Most of us have suffered from such people, who are apt to gather at such resorts as residential hotels. They were generally quite unable to amuse themselves and lived lives of unprofitable boredom, a nuisance to themselves and to most people whom they met.[17]

The Tourist Family

For the emancipated family "relations with the neighborhood are casual, of the 'touch and go' type."[18] This also applies to the tourist family.[19] On the road there are no tele-

---

[16] Thorstein Veblen, *Theory of the Leisure Class* (New York, 1899), p. 171.

[17] *The Case for Capitalism* (New York, 1920), p. 28.

[18] Ernest R. Mowrer, *The Family* (Chicago, 1932), p. 98.

[19] Mobility has been defined by R. D. McKenzie as movement that involves a change of residence and fluidity as movement without change in residence. Families vary in mobility from the stable family, living permanently in one place, to the migrant family; and in fluidity, from the family with a narrow geographical range to the tourist family.

phone calls, no door bells and no committee meetings. Community contacts are temporary and fleeting. At least for the duration of the tour the family is emancipated.

The family at home lives according to a more or less established routine. There tends to be a schedule for work and play. When the family travels, however, this routine is broken and habitual forms of behavior must be modified. Under these circumstances it is difficult if not impossible to maintain a fixed schedule. Novel situations necessitate changes in family customs which sometimes create restlessness and a feeling of insecurity.

At home each member of the organized or integrated family plays a rôle in the family interaction and this rôle is defined by the attitudes of the other members.[20] When the family is touring characteristic changes tend to occur in these rôles and in the relationships between the different members. When the man takes a vacation from work his wife frequently feels that she should have a vacation too, and as a result even in tourist camps the trend seems to be away from cooking and toward more "hotel service," i.e., having the beds made up in advance and the linen furnished. In the words of one auto camp owner an increasing number of his guests "don't carry a thing—only cigarettes" and those parties that do cook commonly "buy a little stuff for supper—'coffee and' for breakfast and away they go."

The patron is more likely to bring his family with him to an auto camp than to a hotel. Studies of auto campers in the Puget Sound region and in Southern California showed that more than 90 per cent were present in family groups. Only 16 per cent of 10,961 Seattle hotel dwellers were living in family groups. In both auto camp and hotel the dominant type of family is the couple without children.

A cottage for transients duplicates the home situation

[20] Burgess, "The Family as a Unity of Interacting Personalities, *The Family*, March, 1926.

more closely than a hotel room and is less expensive. The tourist is close to his car and baggage and his wife can prepare the meals. The hotel on the other hand appeals to people who want comfort and do not wish to set a house to rights or cook their own meals.

The studies cited above showed a proportion of children among auto campers about eight times as great as among hotel dwellers and about four-fifths as great as in the general population, but they also revealed more than twice as large a percentage of elderly people in the hotels as in the auto camps. People with children seem to appreciate the economy and freedom of life in auto courts while the older folk seek the comfort and ease of the hotel home. Although the sanitary arrangements in cottages for transients frequently leave much to be desired, there is more likely to be an opportunity for children to play out-of-doors and there is no necessity that they stay "dressed up" as in a city hostelry. After the average trip of 250 to 300 miles children jump out of the car and are all over camp in a short time. The chance for spontaneous play in travel-worn clothing is especially desirable after being pent up during hours of driving.

In the locality of permanent residence each member of the family has contacts outside of the home group which play a more or less important part in his life. On the tour these contacts are cut off and the family itself becomes the social world for each member. Life in the large commercial cabin camp located on an arterial auto route tends to be almost as transient and impersonal as in the "grand caravansery" of the metropolis.[21] One's neighbor is merely a noise. The resulting social self-sufficiency of the family group, especially when accentuated by travel fatigue, tends to place a strain on the family solidarity. On the other hand, the

---

[21] Human relations in the small cottage court located on a beach at an objective point for vacationing tend to be less formal and external and are analogous to those in the small resort hotel.

narrowness of interests within the family circle with its consequent conflict and boredom may be offset to some extent by the new sights and strange adventures jointly shared by all individuals in the party.

CHAPTER IX

THE HOTEL CHILD

A GAY LITTLE LASS of four, arrayed in a bright yellow dress danced out from a corridor into the lobby of a large residential hotel. She paused in front of three grinning bellboys just long enough to stand on her head and then pretended to jump into the fountain.

All children have, of course, a desire to be recognized and approved by their playmates and elders, but in the case of most hotel children this wish is exaggerated. In fact the presence of children in hotels is sufficiently unusual in itself to attract attention. Although it is clear that the proportion is larger in residential than in transient hotels there is no accurate nation-wide data on the subject. The fact that the percentage of children is nine times as great in the general population of Seattle as in its hotel population is suggestive. Because of this relatively small number, children are more noticeable in the hotel and are more likely to behave in ways that bring applause than children in a less conspicuous environment. Occasionally one finds a well-mannered, apparently wholesome hotel child. In these exceptional cases, however, the child is not permitted the run of the hotel and his activities are very carefully supervised and controlled. The little "actor" or "actress" is more characteristic.

In the leading commercial house of a small city there was only one child, an attractive, black-haired girl. She rode up and down in the elevators continually. Men in the lobby, who were total strangers, bought things to amuse her. She fared so well with them, in fact, that she would have nothing to do with women. Although three months of living in the hotel had made this three-year-old much bolder, still her mother did not seem to care.

When another hotel product was in high school at the early age of twelve, she took special pains to study her Latin in the lobby where people would notice and comment on her precocity. Once she asked the house physician the meaning of a Latin word in order to answer his surprised question by explaining that she was in high school although only twelve years old. Not only had this young lady lived at a residential hotel for three years, she had also accompanied her father on business trips which necessitated staying at many different hotels, from the St. Francis in San Francisco to the Knickerbocker in New York. While stopping at the latter hotel she occupied a room adjacent to Caruso's, made friends with the great tenor and proudly told her acquaintances, "Caruso sang for me this morning." At the present time, although no longer living in hotels, she is a very urbane and sophisticated young woman.

Irene, at seven, had the manner of a stage child. She wore a pink chiffon frock, silk stockings and pink satin slippers. With Doris, her little friend, she talked to the office clerks and the bellboys, watched a new elevator man and commented admiringly on a lady in a flame colored dinner gown and smart black hat. A man crossed the lobby. "Why, there is Irene, my little sweetheart," he said. Irene threw back her head with a haughty air and walked over to a far corner, all with the manner of a woman of twenty. "Then I will have Doris," he laughed, and there followed a few moments of thoroughly grown-up acting.

On a rainy holiday I found Doris, the leader of the little girls, starting something in the small sun parlor where they often gather. "Now you all run and get the pillows and we will play," she ordered. The girls came back quickly with about a dozen silk and tapestry pillows, the only movable furnishings in the lounge. These were placed on the floor while Doris directed. One child was the nurse, the other three were children and Doris was the mother. Doris had only one offspring and the other two youngsters were visitors. She instructed her child, "Now you must be very bad and we will play your father travels and you are very much afraid of him. I will lie down and you all be very bad."

Doris reclined on the pillows and the little girls proceeded to become very noisy. She complained in vain that they must behave. She called the nurse to account: "Nurse, you must keep them quiet. I want to sleep. I cannot bother with them. You must attend to it, nurse." To her own child she said, "Your father is coming home Christmas and I will tell him how bad you have been and then you will be sorry."[1]

It is quite generally agreed that "the hotel is a poor place for children," but not all cliff dwellers are as frank as the mother who confessed: "I raised two boys in a hotel and did a rotten job of it." For one thing she had difficulty in making George take a bath. When she attempted it, George, who had a slight but harmless palpitation of the heart, would yell, "Mother, my heart, my heart!" and she would desist, fearing lest persons in adjacent rooms be disturbed and think her cruel. She also found it hard to "keep track of" the children and was continually sending a bellboy after them. George lived with his parents in a hotel while the other son, Fred, was away at school much of the time. Since his mother was "too lazy to get up," George usually ate his breakfast alone. In the evening she frequently went out with her husband leaving the boy, who was not old enough to go out by himself, alone in the hotel rooms. He usually read or studied while his father and mother were away but often became very lonesome. "Won't you get somebody to stay with me?" he once asked a neighbor who was attracted by his crying. Now, at twenty-two, he is a traveling salesman, likes excitement and change and thinks that life must

[1] From the observations of a guest in a residential house.

be very dull for his mother because she lives in an apartment house. Fred, on the other hand, has married and is ardently devoted to life in his own home.

Practically all of Ann's seventeen years had been spent in hotels and she spoke about hotel life in no uncertain terms. She could not think of a single virtue that it had for a child. Four reasons were advanced for disapproval : (1) It is hard for a hotel child to have friends his own age, not merely because of mobility, but also because outside children seem to fear hotels. (2) There is not enough exercise and fresh air. (3) It is bad to eat out all the time. The food may be all right, but contacts with the public are not so good. (4) The child has too much association with older people. She summarized her attitude by saying emphatically, "I will never marry a hotel man and I will never raise a child in a hotel."

Eleanor, age three, had never known any other home than a hotel room. Her mother was very busy socially ; her father, the hotel manager, only used his rooms to sleep in and to change his clothes. Any discipline had to be exerted in a way that would not make her cry, for that would disturb the neighbors. Consequently it consisted chiefly of preventing occasions that would make it necessary, and Eleanor usually had her own way.

She ate breakfast in the Grill—there were not many patrons at that time. Her lunch and dinner were brought to her room on a tray. At first her mother telephoned the dining room before each meal and ordered the food, but finally she decided that the house-boy "seemed to know what children should eat," so she paid him by the month to order and deliver Eleanor's meals!

Although the child was seldom allowed in any part of the hotel except her own room, she was at home any place in the building. In the morning she would finish her breakfast before the rest of us and climb down from her chair. Then she would run from one table to another receiving a good deal of attention from everyone. The cashier gave her life-savers and many people asked her questions. By the time we had finished breakfast she would be out in the hall having a glorious time talking to the colored shoe-shiner. As she passed through the lobby the telephone girl, desk clerk and bellboys spoke to her and she called them all by their first names. She knew the many permanent guests and was greeted by all of them.

Under these circumstances Eleanor's lack of self-consciousness was remarkable. I have never seen her show off, or do anything smart-aleck-like. She is as natural and unaffected as any child I ever saw. The thing that has saved her from being terribly spoiled is that she is an extrovert and is always so intensely interested in objective things that she has no time to become self-conscious. The only ill effect of her contacts with the public was in making her independent to the point of stubbornness. Her mother never made any attempt at discipline in public. She let her do exactly as she pleased, because, when reprimanded, Eleanor always made a scene and that was one thing that her mother wanted to avoid at all costs.

Eleanor's best friends among the employees were Joe, the head bellboy, and Susie, the chambermaid. Toward Joe she displayed the greatest awe, respect and admiration, partially because of his red and gold uniform, but also because of his pleasant disposition. When Joe came into the apartment Eleanor invariably ran to meet him. He was the only person to have that distinction. She was always more excited about a visit from him than from her father. Her attitude toward Susie was entirely different, however. Susie was the one person who was completely subordinate. She was the grey-haired, eternally tired and apologetic type of chambermaid that one sees in the movies. The child ordered her about like a young tyrant. At any time during the day when we would ask Eleanor to pick up her toys, blocks, mittens or rubbers she would say with great unconcern, "Susie will pick up them."

She was constantly with older people. Her mother had guests nearly every day, either a group for bridge in the afternoon, or a cocktail party before dinner in the evening. These people were young, and few of them had children of their own, so Eleanor was a great attraction. She was also on friendly terms with the family bootlegger. She was well acquainted with the type of merchandise he handled. Her parents talked to her just as they would to an adult and never made any attempt to conceal their cocktails, cigarettes, off-color stories or Ballyhoo magazines.

Eleanor's mother did not approve of rearing a child in a hotel. She considered it an unfortunate but necessary aspect of her husband's occupation.[2]

Eleanor's independent ways dramatize a tendency, seen in many urban children, to "define the situation" for themselves, i.e., to do as they please. When this "individualization of behavior" expresses itself in such pranks as dropping firecrackers on the passersby in the street below, it creates a problem for the management.

Children, unless they were exceptionally well behaved, were the despair of the hotel manager, and yet what could the management do when one mother complained that the clerk in the office had scolded her "darling boy" for yelling in the lobby? He had always done exactly what he pleased and would continue to do so. Or what could they do when a small girl deliberately walked all over the grand piano and was never scolded by her "doting" mother? So these children and many others continued to act like little hoydens, and generally marred and ruined the furniture and decorations of the lobby and their own rooms. One family living across from us had two boys, and they were actually insulted when the manager told them the boys would have to be kept from swearing in the presence of the ladies in the lobby. The mother said her boys had never uttered a bad word, but how was she to know what they did and said when she was shopping, playing bridge or at her club all of the time?[3]

It is interesting that the children from two Jewish families in this hotel were "beautifully brought up and ranked much above many gentile children in manners and obedience." Jews, more than other nationalities, seem to have developed controls that enable them to live contentedly in a highly

---

[2] Adapted from a paper written by Eleanor's nursemaid.
[3] "Two Years in a Residential Hotel."

urbanized environment. Since those medieval times when they were forced to live in city ghettos Jews have become more and more adjusted to a metropolitan existence. In general the larger the American city, the greater their proportion in the population—about 25 per cent in New York, 10 per cent in Chicago and 4 per cent in Seattle. Although no statistics are available on the subject, it is probably true that the percentage of Jews among the hotel dwellers of a city is always larger than their ratio in the general population of the same community.

Mr. and Mrs. Bernstein with their two boys, one three and the other nine, have lived in a large residential hotel for three years. They moved to the hotel from a less desirable neighborhood at an increase of about fifty dollars a week in expense. The rental for the suite which they now occupy is seven hundred dollars a month. Mrs. Bernstein moved under protest, but she now thinks that home life was increased by the change. Previously her husband, who has a large amount of "nervous energy" and who must be continuously on the go, would stay at home perhaps fifteen minutes, and then they must visit somebody, go to the theatre, do something. Now he can go down into the lobby after dinner, and she can stay and play with her boys, joining him later. At first it was hard to get the older boy, who is too big for the nurse to look after, out of the apartment. Now it is hard to keep him in. He was recently caught trying to open the door to an elevator shaft and has gotten into other troubles. Another boy in the hotel is thought to be a "vicious influence."

Mrs. Israel has lived in a hotel with her son for ten years and does not want a home of her own. If, occasionally, the son becomes pent up, irritable and restless, she takes him away to a springs or a mountain resort. He is himself again in a few days or a week. His ability to make friends easily, and his more mature attitude toward problems in general she attributes to hotel life. The greatest strain in his development has been due to the myriad of questions asked him by guests in the lobby. It is her conclusion that "hotel life and contacts broaden children."

Like the Bernsteins and Israels some families with children are more or less accommodated to hotel life. They prefer it to any other domicile status and are usually permanent guests. Other families who live with children in hotels are not adapted to this mobile environment. They idealize life in their own homes and are frequently, but not always, temporary visitors.

To the latter type belongs the Ambrose family. This group has lived two and a half months in a San Francisco apartment hotel and in other hostels for shorter periods. During twenty-five years of married life thay have owned their own home for sixteen. They do not want to make their home in a hotel while the three children are with them. Although it is cheaper in the transient abode they much prefer the individual home.

There is less freedom in a hotel. Music must stop at 10:30. You must tell your friends not to enjoy their jokes with such glee. Your clothes are so crowded you can never find anything. A home is much better. The mother has more responsibility in a hotel, for she has a harder time making her family happy. The unsettled feeling of living in a hotel makes us all discontented.

The difficulty that parents commonly experience in providing adequate recreation for children under the congested conditions of hotel existence is seen in the following adventures of a home-owning family.

I shall always have vivid memories of our six weeks in a Los Angeles apartment hotel. The structure was a new, snappy, five-story edifice with 56 suites—doubles, singles, bachelor quarters and one master suite. Since it was summer time and the quiet season, the management had rented us an apartment in spite of our two offspring. We were on the ground floor where running would not matter so much and the children would not need to be rescued from the elevator.

Housekeeping was easy. There was an abundance of fresh linens and hot water. Refrigeration, janitor and maid service were included. I should have been a lady of leisure. But alas! What to do with two lively youngsters in three rooms, kitchenette and bath!

The city sweltered through three weeks of "very unusual weather." All windows were wide open to invite just a wisp of breeze. We were too near our neighbors to permit crying or noisy play. One morning at 10:30, the neighbor who kept us awake until 2:00 or 3:00 a.m. twice a week with her loud parties screamed out at Son across the small court, "Will you shut up, you blankety blank?" And to her companion, "Those terrible children drive me frantic."

During the day I kept the children away from the hotel as much as possible. We made many half-day excursions to the beach or about town. At other times, with no park or playground near, we resorted to frequent short walks in the blazing sun. We bounced balls on the sidewalks. But it was an area of few children and stepping on a lawn to retrieve a ball might arouse a glassy stare from the householder. Once little Daughter climbed a sturdy tree in a parking strip. A woman, who didn't see me, bellowed from the porch, "Get out of that tree!" I became super-sensitive about the children's actions and went with them everywhere.

The hotel was very noisy and we didn't make all of it. There was a stream of automobile traffic on our street with the grinding of brakes for a stop light at the next corner. Paper boys thoughtlessly chatted near our windows at 5:30 a.m. Blatting radios were not always silenced at 11:00 p.m., and on some Saturday nights there were drinking parties on both sides of us.[4]

But the extent to which the human organism can adapt itself to noise is remarkable. Two daughters of a Boniface, for whom it is a strange adventure to stay in a house, are disturbed by the absence of noise on the street. "In the country even a cricket, or just the stillness, will keep me awake," said a barber, whose room in a cheap hotel is located next to the roar of the elevated.

---

[4] Una Middleton Hayner.

In the Los Angeles experience there were no rainy days. During stormy weather, permanent guests with children cannot take them to the park. Cooped up within the small walled space of a hotel room, they are little better off than animals in a zoo. The individual house has stairs to climb, the basement and attic to explore, a kitchen and a garage. Nearby are the homes of neighbors. Even Mine Host sometimes finds it necessary to move his family to a separate dwelling.

I was born in a Yakima hotel, the sixth child in a growing family. Several bedrooms and a kitchenette were set aside for our use. My father owned the hotel; my mother and the older girls helped him as housekeeper and chambermaids. Finally, with the family still increasing, the folks decided it would be better to move into a home. There were not enough play spaces, it was too much trouble to make us be quiet and we were coming in contact with the wrong kind of people.

The influence of hotel life on the developing personality is well illustrated in "The True Story of a Hotel Child."[5] Although the writer of this article calls herself a child she is really twenty-seven years old, "and even for twenty-seven I have the maturity and poise that living in public gives both men and women." "What I am is a hotel child," she continues. "I am a product of the hotel, just as surely as one speaks of a Southerner or New Englander, or as a girl bears the imprint of a certain school or college." She continues:

Only three times have we had what could be called a home of our own. Three different times we rented a furnished house; and I will say that the servant problem, and the general discomfort which resulted from my mother and myself not knowing how to cope with the situation, make housekeeping seem much less homelike than when we go back to some hotel where we

[5] "The True Story of a Hotel Child—An Autobiography," *The Designer*, April, 1922.

have the same suite that we are accustomed to and where we are waited on by willing bellboys and smiling chambermaids whose comings and goings do not disturb the economy of our family.[6]

Eating in the public dining room alone, playing in the corridors and parlors, "all but sleeping in public," gave this child a composure and urbanity far beyond her years. There were kisses from strange gentlemen in the lobby; trips through private rooms with a talkative chambermaid; feelings of shyness at the critical faces and new teachers in different private schools, followed by periods of inadequate and irregular tutoring at the hotel; friends for a week or two, most of whom she never saw again; and for her mother and herself—the father had his business connections—the distances that come from "being an outsider everywhere."

One is dependent on people as those who live in homes of their own never are. There is no round of duties except what one makes artificially. The days slip by useless and empty, and the worst of it is one gets used to the emptiness and likes it.[7]

In an attempt to meet some of the problems suggested above a number of hotels have special dining rooms for children where mothers or maids may take the youngsters for their meals rather than into the more formal dining room or coffee shop. Conditions may be "even worse" in such an eating place, one critic complains, because of the "talk and jokes that pass between the waiters and nurses." The recreation room or playground, another method of control, is coming to be regarded as standard equipment in the larger hotels.

My personal opinion is that commercial hotels over 500 rooms in size, large resort hotels and all residential hotels should have their own play rooms or play grounds. There are exceptions in

---

[6] *Ibid.*　　　　[7] *Ibid.*

hotels that now cater to a small percentage of family trade or that do not feel that this percentage can be increased.[8]

The energetic manager of an important beach resort remarked that children present the "biggest problem any hotel has to face." He employs a trained kindergartner who helps to educate the fifty or sixty children under her care, in addition to giving them a good time. Besides the beach he has a park and an indoor play room. The youngsters have developed a kind of city government among themselves with a mayor, a city council and a chief of police. They inflict punishment upon themselves.

Such experiments as these are no doubt helpful administrative devices and should be encouraged, but they are obviously inadequate to meet the problem in a fundamental way. The difficulty is something more than "keeping the children from the corridors and disturbing the general peace." It is more, in other words, than a problem in management. It is a question of youthful, plastic human nature under the influence of an extreme and exaggerated form of city life. The hotel child is, after all, only an accentuation of the city child, and juveniles in the great city tend to become adolescents socially while they are still pre-adolescents physiologically. The resulting product is a type much more sophisticated than the farm-bred child of an earlier day.

Charles J. Galpin argues, for example, that "the individual freedom of the country child to grow and expand his physical capacity, unchecked, is paralleled on the psychical side by a freedom from the crowding congestion of personalities found in the metropolitan centers."[9] Since 1918, when he published his statement, even the country has been experiencing radical changes under the influence of modern means of transportation and communication. At the present

---

[8] J. O. Dahl, "When Does a Play Room Become a Profitable Investment," *Hotel Management*, November, 1925.

[9] *Rural Life* (New York, 1918), p. 121.

time parents in the village and to some extent in the open country are meeting problems involved in the growing urbanization of American life.

In short, the problem of the hotel child is bound up with the nature of metropolitan society and cannot be expected to change radically until the conditions that give rise to it are changed.

PART III

BEHAVIOR AWAY FROM HOME

CHAPTER X

THE LURE OF HIGHWAYS AND CITY LIGHTS

In the United States a fashion was set by George Washington and his contemporaries of going to a watering place —sometimes ten days distant—in quest of health. Although climate and medicinal waters were then advocated only for their value in connection with definite health problems, a twinge in the toe might be a satisfactory alibi and Bourbon whiskey might take the place of mineral water at the springs. Before the Civil War the leading resort hotels were located at Saratoga Springs in New York, at White Sulphur Springs in West Virginia and in the White Mountains of New Hampshire. One is impressed by the narrow geographical range of early vacationists. Europe was relatively inaccessible, although popular with the rich, and Florida was still undeveloped as an American Riviera. People were so busy settling the country and earning a living that winter, fall and spring resorts were unknown. Few could take a vacation in the summer. "As the country became more prosperous, the leisure class increased in numbers and now even the busiest man realizes that he must take time for recreation at different seasons of the year."[1]

The early resorts were made accessible by steamship or railroad, often supplemented by stage coach, as in the Yellowstone as late as 1916. Atlantic City had its beginning as a leading convention and recreation center when a railroad was built from Philadelphia. In 1909 a railroad was extended southward from St. Augustine opening up successively Palm

---

[1] E. L. Potter (President, Clarendon Hotel, Seabreeze, Florida), "Operating American Resort Hotels," *Hotel Management*, January, 1923, p. 26.

Beach, Miami and Key West. By 1922 a writer in the *Saturday Evening Post* describes "the time killer industry at Palm Beach, Florida, where people who have more money than they need spend their time industriously as society climbers, fashion plates, scandal mongers, whiskey guzzlers and gamblers."[2] In its 1912 compilation from recreation booklets the *Literary Digest* stressed railroad connections to American mountain and inland resorts. In 1913 it featured inland waterways, lake and river steamers. This emphasis is not seen in later compilations.

With the beginning of the Great War in 1914 the blocking of American trips to European resorts encouraged development of equivalent facilities in recreation areas of the United States. At first most of the longer trips were by train. An article in the May 1912 issue of *Travel* describes a pioneer motor tour to the Pacific Coast and back in the "Mud Hen." The experiences on this tour are an index to the crudities of motor travel at that time. Even in 1916 travel across Indiana, Illinois, Iowa and Nebraska—states that now have a network of paved highways—was practically impossible after a rain because of the sticky "gumbo." Between 1922 and 1930, however, automobiles had entered the picture sufficiently so that the number of persons arriving by rail at Yellowstone National Park showed no upward trend. During the same nine-year period automobile arrivals increased about three fold. In general the shorter the distance from which guests came to the park the greater the likelihood that they would come by motor car.

In response to this growing importance of the automobile many resort areas in the United States have experienced radical changes. The development of Long Beach Peninsula on the coast of the State of Washington may be taken as an example.

[2] See article headed "The Industrious Time Killers" in the *Hotel Monthly* for May, 1922.

The first white family arrived at the site of Ilwaco on the Columbia River in 1859. The doors of their home were open to all travelers. For about thirty years communication from Ilwaco to points on the Peninsula's twenty-six miles of sand beach was either on foot, by horse and wagon or by stage, using crude wagon roads. Although a few persons were spending their summers on the beach as early as 1879, the Peninsula was not made accessible as a resort area until 1889. In that year a narrow gauge railroad that connected with a stern-wheeler from Portland, Oregon, was completed. During this second period in the evolution of the area visitors usually came in family groups, built cottages at the beach and stayed during the entire summer.

A fundamental change took place with the shift from rail to automobile transportation. Wagon roads were gradually replaced by gravel highways which were eventually paved. In 1929 the railway was completely dismantled. The average length of stay for the new type of tourist is probably less than a week. There seems to be a smaller proportion of families with children and an increase in married couples without children. Highways have been opened to Puget Sound so that Seattle now vies with Portland as a source of patronage. To the seven resort hotels have been added about thirty automobile tourist courts. It is estimated that 70,000 people visited the beach during the 1933 season.

With the rise of automobile touring contacts between guests have also changed in character. The difference between the intimate and friendly relations in a small New England resort hotel of the older type and the impersonality of the newer and larger hotel with its tourist and "profiteer" trade is strikingly illustrated in the following experience of a middle western university professor.

In all but five of the last thirty summers Professor Colby has spent a month or six weeks at a resort hotel in the White Mountains. Until 1916 he went to a five-hundred room hotel which catered to guests who would remain at least a month. In this hotel the professor and his wife made two hundred acquaintances whom they were in the habit of remembering at Christmas time and whom he still remembers in this way although his wife is no longer living. There were many families and many children among the guests.

But this hotel is on one of the main touring highways. With the beginning of the World War, which precluded European travel, and much to the disgust of the permanent guests, an increasing stream of automobiles with overnight patrons stopped in front of the veranda. The management began definitely to encourage this transient trade. About three-quarters of a mile away a new and larger hotel was built and to this Professor Colby has gone since 1916.

As many as one hundred autos a day arrived at the larger hotel. With the increase in transiency a correlative decrease in the number of children was noted. Whereas formerly the majority of the guests were of the most substantial business type, congenial people whom the professor enjoyed meeting, recently the population has been largely of the profiteer type—men who call themselves financiers or brokers. Many of these profiteers preferred to spend their time in the basement listening to stock tickers rather than out-of-doors in the fresh air. Although he has met others in this hotel, Professor Colby has only made one friend here with whom he corresponds—the man who always won the golf championship. Room rates advanced so noticeably that it was evident the management was catering to persons with money. The last time he was there, the professor had to pay eight dollars a day for a room without bath or twelve dollars, with bath.

That the national parks in the United States were visited by 1,200,000 private automobiles in 1935 is one of the many indices to the extent of American tourism. But how much did the occupants of these cars really see? An interesting observation on the psychology of the "tourist horde" was included in a letter from an auto camp owner in southern Oregon.

Post cards written home by the average traveler show that the main topic is how many miles were covered for the day and how many he expects to make the next day. A comfortable clean place to stop is of secondary importance, and very seldom is any mention made of any scenery passed through. He did not see it, traveling 40 to 50 miles per hour.

There were, of course, travelers in search of recreation long before the days of George Washington and the current vogue of "touring and tripping." Crowds visited spacious health resorts in Ancient Greece and tourists traveled to historic places and studied foreign peoples in the Roman Empire.[3] "With the coming of the stage coach, the frequency of tours—usually through France and Italy with an occasional adventure into Germany or Switzerland—caused the creation of a new expression and a new recreation for wealthy Englishmen in the eighteenth century," writes Robert B. Ludy. "This was the Grand Tour."[4] In his interesting book on *The Grand Tour in the Eighteenth Century* William E. Mead stresses the "great variety in the character of the accommodations to be found in different parts of the Continent. Holland, with its dense population, its standards of neatness and its diffused wealth, is at one extreme, and Italy, with its medieval hill towns affording filthy beds and uneatable food, is at the other."[5]

In the nineteenth century Englishmen were still making the Grand Tour, but they usually made it in a railway coach. In 1844 rail transportation was available between Ostend and Cologne. By 1845 the line from Heidelberg had been

[3] E. L. Sarkies, *The Importance of the Hotel Industry*, pp. 23 and 26. In *Gallus or Roman Scenes of the Time of Augustus* (translated in 1844), Frederick Metcalf makes the following statement about the resort at Baeae: "Besides invalids who hoped to obtain relief from the healing springs and warm sulphurous baths, there streamed thither a much larger number of persons in health, having no other end in view than the pursuit of pleasure, and who, leaving behind them the cares and formalities of life, resigned themselves wholly to enjoyment in whatever shape it was offered." [Quoted by Ernest R. Groves and Lee M. Brooks in their *Readings in the Family* (Philadelphia, 1934), p. 81].

[4] *Historic Hotels of the World*, p. 76.

[5] *Ibid.*

extended as far south as Freiburg. Between Cologne and Heidelberg, however, the popular tourist route was by boat along the Rhine. In August 1844 an American traveler wrote as follows about this trip :

Above Coblenz almost every mountain has a ruin and a legend. I sat upon the deck the whole afternoon, as mountains, towns, and castles passed by on either side, watching them with a feeling of the most enthusiastic enjoyment. Every place was familiar to me in memory, and they seemed like friends I had long communed with in spirit and now met face to face. The English tourists, with whom the deck was covered, seemed interested too, but in a different manner. With Murray's Handbook open in their hands, they sat and read about the very towns and towers they were passing, scarcely lifting their eyes to the real scenes, except now and then, to observe that it was "very nice."[6]

The Swiss hotelkeepers, catering as they did to tourists in search of recreation, are said to have invented the resort hotel. They also pioneered in selling mountain scenery.[7] In 1927 the largest proportion of visitors to this trilingual "playground" were English-speaking. For the depression year of 1931 the number from Germany exceeded the total from England and America.[8] In the same year the French were the most frequent foreign visitors at French-speaking Geneva ; the English, at French-speaking Montreux ; Americans, at German-speaking Interlaken and Germans, at Italian-speaking Locarno. The Swiss themselves, it is interesting to note, visit their own resorts more frequently than any for-

---

[6] Bayard Taylor, *Views A-foot; or Europe Seen with Knapsack and Staff*, pp. 98-99.

[7] "The taste of travelers before the middle of the eighteenth century did not incline toward rough and precipitous scenery, but toward the softer beauties of the verdant plain, the quiet lake, and the mossy dell."—W. E. Mead, *op. cit.*

[8] By remaining on the gold standard Switzerland has come to rank with Holland as one of the most expensive countries in Europe for non-gold standard peoples.

eign nationality.[9] In 1925 visitors from outside countries left more than $80,000,000 in Switzerland—almost enough to cover the excess of imports over exports.

Monsieur Valad is manager of an attractive residential hotel from whose roof garden the guest looks over the winding streets of Geneva to *Lac Leman* and the white tip of Mont Blanc. Since no outsiders are permitted in the lounge, visitors are scrutinized inquisitively by the porter. On the walls of the diplomatic director's office are charts showing the trend of his business and the sources of his patronage over a period of years.

May, August and September are the best months for transient guests. Americans come in August; French at the end of July or the beginning of August; English in April—their Easter vacation lasts a fortnight. The Swiss are also good patrons, but the Germans are not important. Winter sees an almost entirely permanent population in the hotel. In both winter and summer there are twice as many women as men.

The hotel business of Switzerland is down this year (1933) every month as compared with last year. In this hotel the average percentage of occupancy is only about fifty. Some of the downtown hotels are running with six or seven guests and seventy-five servants. There is a great deal of price cutting.

Motoring, as in the United States, has made a big difference in the average length of stay for transient guests. Many tourists now stop in Geneva only one night. The average for the city is three; it used to be eight. Italians, especially, shoot through the city in their big cars. Montreux has been hit very hard by the motor. There are no places to drive to; it is only satisfactory if you walk.

As M. Valad suggests, the Grand Tour of the twentieth century is increasingly by motor car. It is also being made by many tourists from the United States as well as from England. The American Automobile Association, which is

---

[9] Schweizerische Verkehrszentrale, *Der Fremdenverkehr 1931 in der Schweiz.*

authorized to issue *carnets des passages en douane* permitting automobiles imported for touring purposes only to pass through customs without payment of duty, "estimates that nearly 5,000 American cars were shipped abroad in 1930 under this arrangement."[10]

An American driving on the Continent for the first time soon learns to be cautious. Half the speed he uses in the States is fast enough. He misses much that is interesting and charming if he drives too fast; he also takes chances. Many roads, especially in Alpine countries like Switzerland and Austria, are narrow and winding. Except in the larger cities the highway is also the sidewalk for pedestrians. Neighbors stop for a morning chat on the village street. Peasants walk to and from their fields. A workman scratches his foot directly in front of the honking car. Careless dogs still live on in amazing numbers. Donkey carts and oxen prefer the middle of the road. There are no stop signs for traffic coming onto the highway.

But of all the driving hazards in Europe, bicycles are the worst. Cyclists pedal abreast for companionability. They shoot across a main thoroughfare with never a look. They manipulate a U-turn directly in front of the car. In Holland there are four bicycles to every seven persons. Even Queen Wilhelmina rides her *fiets* almost daily. On his second day in France one American motorist only missed running into a boy on a bicycle by driving his car off the highway into a ditch.

Motor touring on the Continent presents other differences. Although Shell or Standard gasoline is available, the ever-present service station as we know it in America is absent. At infrequent intervals, in a public square or outside some shop, there will be a small pump containing *Benzin* or *l'essence*. Women usually work these pumps. If you ask for it, the radiator is filled from a can. Nowhere in a recent 5,000 mile

---

[10] Willey and Rice, *op. cit.*, p. 88.

tour of Western Europe[11] did it occur to any pump operator to clean off the windshield. Distilled water for the battery must be purchased from the *Apoteke* or drug store!

Car owners in France, Italy and Austria like to lean on their horns. In villages, near narrow corners, the loud tootings of these big horns make raucous reverberations against the old walls.

Germans, as well as Americans, enjoy motor touring; but they are also willing to walk, or ride a bicycle. In the United States there are few open country areas, outside of government parks and forests, where trails are provided for those who like to hike. Through the German countryside, on the other hand, *Fusswege* or footpaths are almost everywhere available. Germans think nothing of covering thirty kilometers in a day on one of their excursions. They commonly stay at modest village hotels where prices are low. Every little town has its *Gasthaus* and the distances between centers are short. The present-day German hiker would agree with the American pedestrian of ninety years ago:

In the country taverns we always found neat, comfortable lodging, and a pleasant, friendly reception from the people. They saluted us, on entering, with "Be you welcome," and on leaving, wished us a pleasant journey and good fortune. The host when he brought us supper or breakfast, lifted his cap, and wished us a good appetite—and when he lighted us to our chambers, left us with "May you sleep well!"[12]

Youth shelters, financed in part by popular tag sales, have been provided for wandering young people. The number of these *Jugendherbergen* in Germany increased from 17 in 1911, caring for 3,000 over-night guests, to 2,318 in 1927, giving 2,655,292 nights of shelter.

---

[11] "Comfortably seated in his motor car the modern tourist can now in a single summer cover far more territory than the eighteenth-century tourist could in his entire three years abroad."—Adapted from Mead, *op. cit.*, p. 171.

[12] Taylor, *op. cit.*, pp. 502-3.

Herr Professor von München and his son, both of whom have an intimate knowledge of Austrian and Bavarian *Baden* and out-door recreations, and have also traveled widely in the United States, spoke as follows about the automobile, *Jugendherbergen* and *Hütten* or mountain shelters:

We Germans stay more in one place. We have comfortable homes and are "rooted" there. You Americans have automobiles and move about. You have one car for every five people; we have one for every hundred people. Since it costs two thousand dollars to buy a car in Germany, only the wealthy have them. This and the many inns already available explain the absence of tourist camps. Hitler has abolished the heavy tax on automobiles, however, and is encouraging the production of a cheap car that will sell for four hundred dollars.

There is usually a couple in charge of the *Jugendherbergen—der Vater und die Mutter*. Boys sleep in one ward; girls in another. All each needs to bring is a sheet—blankets are provided. The charge for lodging is twenty *Pfennig* or about eight cents. An older person may stay in one of these youth shelters if he is the leader of a group; otherwise not.

The *Hütten* are shelters found in the high Alps of both Austria and Switzerland. Here also each visitor carries only a sheet. Services vary greatly in different places. Usually there are only mattresses on the floor; sometimes a few cots. Occasionally provision is made both for housekeeping and the serving of meals. All shelters give better rates to members of the Alpine Club. Some have signs indicating the amount due and this is deposited. In winter the *Hütten* are locked, but members have keys. One must always leave the shelter in as good condition as one finds it; if dirty, in a better condition.

THE AMERICAN HOTEL AS A SOCIAL CENTER

In Washington Irving's *Rip Van Winkle* the bench in front of the village inn is described as the meeting place of a "perpetual club of sages, philosophers and other idle personages." There they gossiped listlessly or told "endless

sleepy stories about nothing." Nicholas Vedder, the landlord of the inn, was a sort of village patriarch whose views
on all matters of discussion were given respectful attention.

During a visit to the United States not so long ago, Gilbert
A. Chesterton, the brilliant English essayist, was impressed
by the public nature of American hotel lobbies. "It is not
merely the Babylonian size and scale of the hotels," he remarked, "but the way they are used that struck me. They
are used almost as public streets, or rather as public squares.
People drift in and out again, while, as a matter of fact,
they have no more to do with the hotel than I have with
Buckingham Palace."

The modern American hotel is, however, something much
more important than a gathering place for lobby loafers.
Like the colonial tavern it is a social center for the community; but its hinterland, for activities as well as guests, is
much wider than that of its simple predecessor. The large
metropolitan caravansery attracts gatherings from the local
community, to be sure, but also from regional, national and
international areas.

Hotels vary of course in the extent to which they serve as
social centers and different types of hotels attract different
kinds of groups. Resort hotels frequently feature golf, swimming, sight-seeing tours, bridge, tea dansants, birthday parties, house movies and dinner dances. Leading residential
hotels often cater to fraternity gatherings, service club luncheons, card parties, alumni reunions, business conferences,
conventions and wedding dinners. No other commercial institution houses such a variety of leisure time activities.

Many guests in family hotels do not utilize the facilities
provided by the management for their leisure time, but have
their own social life outside. People who have moved to the
hotel from their own homes naturally take their recreational
habits with them. They frequently retain the same circle of

friends, clubs and lodges without making any additions because they live in a hotel. When a hotel gives one or more dances a week, these are commonly better patronized by people from the outside—transients and individuals having no definite social position—than by the guests themselves. On the other hand there are hotels, especially during the depression, where the weekly dances help to create among the permanent guests the rudiments of a common life.

Both the recreational opportunities available and the degree to which they are utilized vary with the changing seasons. More activities are provided by the Chicago lake-shore hotels during the summer. There is also at this time more participation in hotel recreation on the part of the guests. Many of the southerners who visit these resorts during the warmer weather are convinced that a season here is a liberal education for their daughters.

To handle the complex social life that attends the various functions which are held at a patrician hotel and to guard both the house and its patrons against any irreparable *faux-pas*, there must be someone behind the scenes with tact, experience, judgment and social understanding. This difficult task seems to be falling more and more to the social hostess. At the Edgewater Beach, a Chicago hotel home, the social hostess tried entertainments, such as a general card game or cotillion, that might draw in all the guests; but this was not at all popular and she abandoned the idea. Since people would not like it she did very little introducing. Her experience revealed the divergence in traditions and ideals among the different groups that patronized this hotel. Just as in a city neighborhood there are many people who do not talk the same language or live in the same social world, so in the hotel similar differences create social distances.

The variety of social types and the divergence of points of view are obviously accentuated in the transient hotel. Here the success of the social hostess is a dubious matter. As an assistant manager expresses it, "they don't mix."

The hostess may have a well defined place in a family or residential hotel, or a resort hotel, but in the commercial house, where the guests are transient and the stay is short, there is but little opportunity for the hostess, unless she be a woman of more than ordinary tact; for many people who travel are particular whom they meet in a social way, and resent being introduced by one stranger to another stranger on slight acquaintance, even though the introductions are managed with the best of motives by the professional "hostess."[13]

By a process of natural selection, the hotel attracts a population which is adapted to a mobile existence, and this population in turn makes the hotel—creates, in other words, the environment in which it lives. "You know," said a hotel dweller, "I just love to be where there's life and city lights." The following excerpt illustrates concretely how an aggregation of individuals peculiarly fitted by temperament and tradition for hotel life have created a milieu in which dazzle, jazz and fashionable gowns are characteristic.

Emotional intensity takes on other manifestations, which are more or less familiar in modern American life. It is rather unexpected to find them in such exaggerated forms among Jewish young people who have a tradition of the extreme opposite. There is the craze for dancing and for jazz which has taken the Jewish young world by storm; there is the vicarious sex orgy of free discussion of psychoanalysis; there is unblushing familiarity between the sexes in word and action; and there is a lavishness in dress and jewels that is overwhelming. I heard one gentile woman who had been to the hotel say that she would never again hanker for a platinum and diamond wrist watch or a platinum bar pin.

In the older group the emotional energy which formerly was

---

[13] *Hotel Monthly*, March, 1922, p. 70.

expended on religion, family and study is now being concentrated on bridge. A competent judge—an employee in the hotel —estimated that there were five hundred bridge games going on in the hotel every evening. (There are 1,000 rooms.) Also there are extravagant parties and ostentatious gifts of flowers and candy and silk lingerie and jewelry. Every birthday and anniversary is celebrated by an expensive social function. Satisfaction is also had in the luxury of smooth running, beautifully appointed limousines. There is competition and rivalry in display of expenditure. This rivalry seems to be one of the things that keeps the whole thing going. The woman in a way has come to be a billboard for the advertising of her husband's wealth—and she seems to take pride in her position. Also there seems to be little effort to proportion the expenditure to the income—unless, indeed, every one of these people has unlimited wealth. This last is doubtful, and the people themselves doubt it of each other. "She's just putting on airs; acts as if she had millions. But she needn't think she can put it over on me! I happen to know how much her husband makes—and, believe me, it isn't as much as she'd have you think!" Such is the comment. The defense of the criticized family itself (when it is discussing finances alone) is "Well, we have to live up to our position, don't we?"[14]

Not only does the hotel attract a type of individual who is adapted to excitement; it also draws novelty seekers who are accustomed to a very different kind of existence. At a recent meeting of a national fraternity, for example, two men sat side by side at the hotel banquet table. They are both faithful church members and have all the virtues of the bourgeoisie, but occasionally they become restless. After a few remarks about the change in nature of these annual reunions—how they used to make speeches, but now they only yell, "Rah, rah"—the conversation turned to hotels. Brother Brown, an elderly gentleman who lives in that outwardly complacent middle class paradise near Chicago known as Oak Park, told how his wife had suddenly ex-

---

[14] From a pre-depression paper on "The Jewish Hotel" by a patron.

claimed, "Charlie, I would like to spend a night in a hotel."
"All right, dear," he had said in reply, "and how about the
theatre too?" And so it was arranged. In response to this,
Brother Smith, a younger man who owns a factory on the
drab West Side of the Windy City, admitted that he and
his wife had frequently spent a week or more at the same
hotel. "We like to dance, and the jazz orchestra they have
there is excellent," he said.

If to people of this type spending a night or a week in a
hotel is an adventure it is even more exciting for the small
town merchant and his wife who go into Chicago for a few
days of shopping or theatre-going. Smaller centers, however,
have their leading hotels and theatres and in a similar way
attract people from the surrounding countryside.

The people in our hotel whom I enjoy most are the bridal
couples. Of course, because La Crosse is not a metropolis, few
of them come, but it is interesting to watch the ones that do.
They act differently from any other guests, and it is easy to
identify them the minute they are seen. They are all country
people coming from very small towns near La Crosse. To spend
several days or a week here is, they think, an ideal sort of honey-
moon. They come into the dining room—almost always the man
first—with a very self-conscious air. Both are wearing new clothes.
After they are seated at a little table for two they study the menu
diligently. The man usually leans over, all devotion, and there
follows a period of anxious consultation over what they shall
order. Each has the attitude of deeply desiring to please the
other. Sometimes they talk ; at other times they merely sit and
gaze lovingly at each other. The woman delights in putting the
sugar in the man's coffee. When the meal is over the man carefully helps the woman on with her coat and they make their
exit, perhaps to go to the theatre.[15]

Like the couples described above many of the visitors to
New York's great hotel center come for a good time. They

---

[15] From a paper by the telephone operator.

11

want something more stimulating than their native villages offer. Here are also travelers with varied backgrounds from all parts of the world. There is a stream of more than 30,000 people registering every week at the ninety hotels in the Times Square district.[16] The relation between the theatres on the Great White Way and this fluctuating hotel population is intimate and significant. To draft a paying audience from this aggregation, and at the same time retain the patronage of the tired business man and the commutors of the great city, necessitates an appeal to fundamental passions. The problem before these theatre managers is similar to that before the editors of metropolitan newspapers in their attempts to increase circulation, and the answer in both cases is the same : make the appeal elementary enough so that every human being will be interested.

Here is an aggregate of people who are in no significant sense a social group. A fluctuating audience, migratory, sundered each one from his habitual community background, gathered from the ends of the world and quickly distributed again—in meeting such an audience the theatrical producer must consider actualities, not possibilities.[17]

The general significance of this situation is that the type of performance which is successful on the Great White Way is passed on to smaller centers. "The million or so Americans who attend 'legitimate' theatres each day are overwhelmingly dependent" on the regular commercial theatres of Broadway. It is not the New York theatre as a whole that "dominates the theatre circuits of the entire country," but the "thoroughly typical Broadway of musical comedy and farce and sartorial melodrama which has for its audience the tired business man and the visiting public of the metrop-

---

[16] See the *World Survey* by the Interchurch World Movement of North America, revised preliminary edition, American volume, p. 53.

[17] John Collier, "The Theatre of Tomorrow," *The Survey*, XXXV (January 1, 1916), 381-85.

olis."[18] Consequently shows that make their appeal to what Professor Thorndyke has called "original nature" are passed on to the rest of the country. Since art is dependent upon a common body of traditions and memories, it is obvious that performances of this kind cannot be artistic. One can find more real art in the East Side Ghetto.

I saw more good literature on the stage in those days while I was sewing sleeves into shirts than I saw in all my subsequent career. While Broadway was giving Ibsen the cold shoulder, the East Side was acclaiming him with wild enthusiasm. I saw "Monna Vanna" on the Bowery before the Broadway type of theatre goer had ever heard the name of Maeterlinck. I made my first acquaintance with Greek tragedy when I had not yet learned how to speak English.[19]

Play activities, like family life, have changed greatly since homestead days. Could anything make a more vivid contrast than the recreations of the pioneer and those of the skyscraper nomads? Under the hard conditions of pioneer life few activities were pursued for their own sake. There was, however, some recreation for the men in the necessary hunting and fishing. There was also considerable fun as a by-product of work. Men raced each other cutting grain with a scythe. Barn raisings, quiltings and corn-huskings were all occasions for neighborhood "bees." When the work had been completed at these gatherings everyone joined in a celebration. The emotionalism of religious gatherings afforded another needed diversion. Nevertheless life was a struggle; and leisure, a rare luxury.[20]

In the absence of nation-wide information about the leisure-time activities of hotel dwellers, a modest Seattle study

---

[18] *Ibid.*

[19] M. E. Ravage, *An American in the Making* (New York and London, 1917), p. 150.

[20] See Newell L. Sims, *Elements of Rural Sociology* (New York, 1928), pp. 375-83.

suggests the contrast with pioneer recreations. Forty middle-aged permanent guests—eighteen men and twenty-two women—reported the play activities in which they had participated during the preceding year of their hotel experience. Leisure reading, going to the movies and listening to the radio, in the order named, were the most popular pastimes; playing card games, watching athletic sports, driving automobiles and social dancing came next; golfing, playing tennis, swimming and hiking were the least favored. Although golf was enjoyed one-third as frequently as leisure reading, the other outdoor sports—tennis, swimming and hiking—had only one-twelfth the popularity. "In the development of American athletic sports, the two rôles of participant and observer have been combined in a very effective manner," according to Professor J. F. Steiner.[21] But in recreation, as in other local affairs, the hotel dweller is more often a spectator than a participant.

One of the permanent guests mentioned above described her technique in meeting the leisure-time problem which life in a hotel presents.

Having little responsibility outside of work hours is conducive to using one's freedom for recreation only. It is very easy to fill one's life with trivial pleasures—a continual round of bridge, shows, evenings at friends. One may become so poverty-stricken within herself, that, unless something special is planned, an evening alone will bore her to death. It is a good idea, I have found, to plan a definite amount of time without a program of entertainment. Life is out of balance if there is no pause between thrills to enjoy a memory of the last and an anticipation of the next.

Last year, with no systematic demand on my leisure, it was all at my own disposal. After a few weeks with every night filled, an unoccupied evening made me feel restless. I tried to analyze the situation. Spoiled by being diverted too much seemed to be

---

[21] *Americans at Play* (New York and London, 1933), p. 101.

the answer. After that I spent a certain number of evenings a week in safe and sane ways—enjoying a new magazine, mending, writing letters. It was a pleasure to do in a reasonable way things that had been done in a hop, skip and jump fashion.

Today "we are everywhere hunting the bluebird of romance and hunting it with automobiles and flying machines."[22] With the growth of cities and the increasing urbanization of life have come a rising standard of living and a marked development of recreation and play facilities. In modern industrial society there is, generally speaking, little chance to combine pleasure with toil. One result of this situation is a "restless search for excitement." Provincial people try to escape the dull routine of their home communities by a holiday jaunt to the bright lights of the metropolitan center. On their quest for adventure an increasing number of urbanites travel far and fast in the opposite direction. "People rush through life and through countries," said the Herr Direktor von Strassburg. "They see more, perhaps, but not as fundamentally."[23]

[22] Robert E. Park, "Community Organization and the Romantic Temper" in Robert E. Park and Ernest W. Burgess, *The City*, pp. 115-18.
[23] See pp. 91-92.

CHAPTER XI

PROBLEMS OF HUMAN NATURE

HOTEL DWELLERS seldom learn to endure things submissively the way people often do in their own homes. Although some are happy-go-lucky and easily satisfied, taken as a whole they are a critical group of people. Many are crabbed and insist on prompt and perfect service. They get that way by continually comparing the hotel administrations of different places. Being away from home may disturb the emotional balance of those transient guests who do not live regularly in hotels, making it easier for them to become excited or angry. Visitors who are both tired and hungry present a difficult combination to please as any house wife knows. In short, hotel employees often have to deal with "human nature in a tantrum."

There are people who leave their manners and even their morals at home when they travel. Others seem to forget to take their wits with them. But there are some whose good breeding is so much a part of them that even the maid who "does" their rooms gives a sigh of regret when she finds that they have gone.[1]

Most of the hotel men who have been successful in the art of pleasing people in all their many moods were not educated in academic institutions. They are "self-made" men trained in the school of experience. The late Ellsworth M. Statler, for example, began his career at the age of nine by working in the "glory hole" or furnace of a glass factory. When he

---

[1] Allison Gray "Queer Things That Hotel Guests Leave—and Take," *American Magazine*, XCVII (January, 1924), 49.

was twelve years old his brother found him a position as bellhop in a hotel and his training in hotel service began. At forty-five he built his first Hotel Statler. It was regarded as fantastic in 1908 that each of his hotel's four hundred and fifty rooms should have running ice-water and a bath with tub or shower. Later these and many other notions that he introduced came to be accepted as standard for the better hotels.

The establishment of university courses in hotel management, notably at Cornell, may make Mine Host of the future as well-rounded intellectually as he was at one time physically. The importance of experience is recognized by the professors, however. During the summer the prospective Bonifaces, many of them sons of hotel men, work in hostelries scattered from Maine to California.

The clever hotel clerk is well dressed and suave, to be sure, but first of all he is a diplomat. The government might well insist that future ministers and ambassadors receive some training behind the desk of a leading caravansery. The first lesson for the new greeter is that the guest is always right, and especially so when wrong. Having learned this he can convince the visitor of almost anything. By studying the subtle gestures of mouths, eyes and hands he learns to tell in advance what reactions to expect from men and women. It is just as important to him that relations between guest and hotel be kept smooth as it is to the foreign minister that attitudes toward his country remain friendly. Since the exigencies of travel are often harsh and disturbing, he soon learns that the chief element in diplomacy is a sympathetic insight that quickly finds a responsive note in the guest.[2]

The excellent manner in which hospitality can be organ-

---

[2] Based on a paper by Lawrence J. Zillman, for nine summers chief clerk at Paradise Inn in Rainier National Park.

ized by a competent staff and its effect on a homesick young woman and her mother are illustrated in the following experience.

When we came our reception was distinctly different from what it would have been at any other of the high-class hotels in this area. At the desk the floor manager and room clerk met us with the most perfect air of welcome—it was neither overdone, nor seemingly assumed, but had the effect of personal interest in the fact that this was to be our home. Our rooms were pleasantly lighted and in the most immaculate condition. On the living-room table was a large and really beautiful basket of chrysanthemums which we enjoyed for ten days—"with the compliments of the Management." The effort to make the rooms seem homelike was so evident that we felt a real gratitude.

Previous to this well planned reception they had decided to secure rooms at another large hostelry. Here their experience had been very different.

We crossed the lobby to the room clerk's corner. Both of the clerks at the desk looked like gamblers—calculating, foxy, suave. They were completely detached, wholly mercenary. We stated our case, interrupted by other guests, bellboys and phone calls. The clerk's manner was mechanically punctilious. Indifference and insincerity resounded loudly above his polite attention. For more important people he would have done his acting with more care and zest. We would occupy two of the less expensive rooms which could be quickly filled if we did not take them. Is this cold pecuniary attitude the keynote of the hotel home? I believe it is.

To the person who is not accustomed to living in hotels tipping is a perplexing problem. He does not know when or how much to tip. He may have a fixed notion that the custom is absurd. The traveler may rest assured, however, that whatever the bellboy, waiter or maid is thinking about, the tip plays a rôle in that thinking. The employee's wage is likely to be so low that he must rely on tips to get a decent living. By means of more or less subtle gestures he lets the guest know his attitude. Together with fashion and "front" these attitudes determine one's status in secondary society.

Front office employees can usually pick out the guest who will tip more liberally than the average. The "rounder" is said to be the bellboy's friend. General appearance, manners, clothes, speech, facial expressions, signature and "hotel attitude," i.e., whether at home or not, tell the experienced employee what type of person the guest is.

As a page it was my favorite pastime to size up the guests as they passed me. Ten-centers or good bait—which were they? The salesman who dresses well and is always spotless and smiling is a good tipper. The cheaper his product, however, the less he will tip. The man who is able to buy good clothing, but wears cheaper apparel is probably a non-tipper. Every school child can pick out a teacher. Her grips are immaculate and she expects them to be handled with care. If you pick up more than one at a time she looks worried. This expression of worry usually tells the boy he has drawn a lemon. It is difficult to describe the exact psychology of the process, but it is sufficient to say that when a bellhop carries your bags he knows whether or not you will tip him.[3]

On the continent of Western Europe it is now a widespread practice in hotels and pensions to make a ten per cent charge for service. Under this system no tipping is necessary. "There are now hundreds of European hotels," wrote Arnold Bennett referring to this custom, "where the visitor does not have to tremble, perpend, meditate, balance pros and cons, weigh one degree of merit against another, and finally endure the reproachful gaze of the forgotten and the underestimated as he steps, like a criminal and a martyr, into the station omnibus."[4]

[3] Adapted from a paper by a young man who had served as a page in a Spokane hotel.

[4] "Private Thoughts on European Hotels," *The Bookman*, LXIV (December, 1926), 397-402.

It is easy to idealize European hotels and service. Any honest traveler can recall unpleasant experiences, such as shaving water delivered in a cream pitcher, supercilious waiters and petty overcharging. But he will also probably sympathize with the following reaction of the widely traveled university professor quoted in chapter I.

Servants abroad seem quite human. Here they are detestable. You feel that as a class they hate and despise the people they are compelled to serve.

The world famous school for hotel employees in Lausanne, Switzerland, takes the position that a hotel man should know the entire business. The prospective manager must be able to make sauces or roasts in the kitchen. He must understand the maturing and proper blending of wines and spirits. He must be able to wait. A good waiter places the menu before the guest, to be sure, but he also tells him very politely what the items are. The English waiter has the reputation for being the worst in Europe, but not worse than the American. His attitude is not right. It is not characteristic of either Britisher or American to be cringing, humble and ingratiating.

SOUVENIR HUNTING

Among the problems of human nature which the hotel manager must combat is souvenir hunting. The "souvenir habit" has been defined by a hotel detective to include "everything from the taking of a carnation from the lobby bouquet to the theft of hundreds of dollars worth of silver and linen at a time."[5] About 2,000 face towels and 300 bath towels a month is the reported loss from Hotel Pennsylvania.

---

[5] Denniston, "Curbing the Souvenir Hunter," *Hotel Management* (May, 1922). For a definition of the term "human nature" see R. E. Park and E. W. Burgess, *Introduction to the Science of Sociology*, pp. 65-68. The sociological interpretation of human nature as a product of group life is similar to the hotel man's use of the term to describe the impulsive behavior of his guests. "The lower animals do not have law and they do not have crime," writes Professor

They take *everything*, except the actual furniture! They take sheets and pillow cases. I have known them to take even a pillow itself.

The men leave the women far behind when it comes to the variety of objects they carry off. I have known men to cut the wires and remove the electric side lights from the walls, or to take the desk lights—silk shades and all. I have known them to take the rug from the floor in front of the dresser, the draperies from the windows, even the framed pictures from the walls!

Some people clean out a writing desk of everything it contains : paper, envelopes, penholders, extra pens, telegraph blanks, laundry lists, blotters—even the ink bottle itself! They take all the soap from the bathroom. Sometimes they take the glass tumblers.

Of course, in the case of soap and stationery, they probably think they have a right to take it. But they certainly have no excuse for taking the permanent fixtures, or the linen, or the blankets.[6]

Guests also leave articles in their rooms when they check out. "Everything from a toothbrush to a fur coat" is included, "but I think the prize ought to be given to the man who went off and left his glass eye on the bureau. The maid received quite a shock when she found it lying there."[7]

A questionnaire sent by *Hotel Management* to "five hundred representative hotels of all classes in all parts of the country" indicates that towels and demi-tasse spoons are the most popular souvenirs. "And strung along down the line, in order of their losses, follow ash trays, light bulbs, sheets, blankets, china, bath mats, butter spreaders and scarves."

Edwin H. Sutherland in his *Criminology* (Philadelphia and London, 1924). "Law-making is distinctively human ; so is law-breaking. Crime is a problem in human nature."

[6] Gray, "Queer Things That Hotel Guests Leave—and Take," *American Magazine*, XCVII (January, 1924), 49. Quoted by permission of the *American Magazine*.

[7] *Ibid*.

One reply recounts an experience with the opening of a new hotel in whose dining service handsomely carved silver pepper and salt shakers, shaped like an egg, served to set off the tables with peculiar touches of charm. But not for long. "In six months," says the writer, "there wasn't a darned one left in the house. You can't stop 'em."[8]

The only thing that one hotel dweller "saved" was stationery. He admitted, as part of his hotel experience—which incidentally was itself written on paper from an important hostelry—that he had in his possession "stationery from eighty-seven different hotels in the United States." At the other extreme of souvenir hunting is the case of a woman who, one morning, with the aid of a rope, lowered everything from her room to the alley below. She then came downstairs, paid her bill and made away with the stolen goods.

Not always does the guest escape however. Two girls filled their hand bags and suit cases with articles from their room. They brought their luggage downstairs and left it with the clerk while they went out for a few minutes. One of the maids discovered the loss from the room. The suit cases were opened. When the girls returned to pay their bill and get their grips, they were caught. Another hotel placed small Oriental rugs in front of the elevators on the various floors. The housekeeper was told to watch that they did not disappear. When she reported one of them missing it was found in a traveling man's room. He said he was "only fooling and didn't mean anything by it."

College students delight in decorating rooms with "souvenirs." An unusual instance involved a large group of college girls. On some special occasion these young women occupied an entire floor of a hotel in Raleigh, North Carolina. After they left, it was discovered that many articles

---

[8] "How to Thwart Hotel Thieves," *Hotel Management*, November, 1922 and January, 1923.

were missing. The manager thereupon sent word to the president of the college from which the girls had come that if the property of the hotel was not returned he would send a private detective to search every room in the dormitories. A special meeting was called in the chapel. The president presented the matter humorously and said that the door to his office would be open at such and such an hour. Three large boxes of towels, sheets, curtains, and even table lamps, were returned to the hotel.

Our house is always supplied with ash trays, smoking stands, spittoons and silverware by brothers lifting them from various hotels and clubs. Among our prizes are a large vase for cigarette butts which was removed under an overcoat and a large brass-topped smoking stand. Our silverware contains pieces from every house on the campus and from many hotels. A scales in our up-stairs lavatory was procured from some drug store. The house mechanic removed the pennies from it and fixed it so they weren't required. We had two cement park benches, but prudence suggested that we put them in the front yard of a rival fraternity and call a prowler car to the scene.[9]

In a wealthy home near New York City a guest noticed various towels and sheets marked with hotel names. When she expressed surprise, her hostess explained that they felt entitled to take such things from hotels since they had to pay such high rates. The taking of towels, soap, or napkins is frequently defended in this way by reference to the high prices paid for hotel rooms. The souvenir, it is argued, is only a slight compensation for being charged too much.

The attitude of the souvenir hunter is naturally quite different from that of the management. Once a hotel manager was entertained in a beautiful home in the best residential section of Rockford, Illinois. While there, his hostess proudly displayed a thermos bottle taken from the Black-

---

[9] From a sociological study of a fraternity.

stone in Chicago and told how she got it. Naturally enough the manager disapproved of her act and urged her to return it. A sign posted in a certain hotel—"Are you a thief? If so, take a souvenir"—indicates clearly the position of most hotel managers. Apparently the women who returned linen and silver taken by them from the St. Francis Hotel in San Francisco about twenty years before had been won over to the management's point of view.[10]

Another method used by hotel men in combating this tendency is illustrated by the story of the young woman who was attending a convention with her husband. Dainty silver sugar bowls graced the dining room tables of the hotel. She expressed a desire for one—to her husband. They got away with it without being detected. On arriving home, however, what was her chagrin when she discovered the engraving on the bottom of the bowl—"stolen from the ——— Hotel."[11]

The larger and more transient the hotel, the greater the souvenir problem tends to be. Such was the finding of the questionnaire sent out by *Hotel Management*. In the residential hotel the guests stay longer and are somewhat known by the management, whereas in a huge metropolitan hostelry, like the New Yorker, the social situation is more impersonal, transitory and anonymous. Taking towels from a large business organization of this sort belongs in a similar moral category to putting something over on the government. Both give the impression of being great wealthy concerns. If one can beat them some way, argues the souvenir hunter, one is just that much ahead.

The landlord of colonial days was held responsible for the character of his guests. Just as the innkeepers in many coun-

---

[10] The manager of a hotel in Redding, California, was not greatly alarmed by the gradual loss over a six-year period of $2,000 worth of silverware. He was very much surprised, however, when a conscience-striken former guest returned by mail $75 worth of plate bearing the hotel monogram.

[11] *Hotel Monthly*, January 1922, p. 64.

tries of Western Europe today must report their visitors to the police,[12] so the Nicholas Vedders of the early American taverns had to give the names of all unknown strangers to the "selectmen, who could, if they deemed them detrimental or likely to become a charge on the community, warn them out of town."[13]

The problem presented to the American landlord of modern times is much more difficult. The same impersonal situation that encourages the souvenir hunter facilitates the activities of the professional criminal.

The impression on the part of the general public that a hotel, its lounges, lobbies, and comfort stations, are for its use and convenience, as well as for that of hotel guests is decidedly a trouble-breeding idea. Twenty-five thousand suburbanites—exclusive of suburban patrons—frequent lobbies of New York hotels without spending five cents in them annually. They form the fog of obscurity in which the crook, thief, coat taker, souvenir grabber, pickpocket, and out and out criminal find security for their mistaken vocation.[14]

The "dead beat" who "skips" without paying his bill is one of the pests that Mine Host is glad to turn over to an officer of the law. Sometimes a "skipper" is clever enough to hang the "Please Do Not Disturb" sign on the door knob so the housekeeper will not discover that he has left. Occasionally a "four flusher" will rent a room; will send his laundry out for which the hotel must pay; and will have his checks in the café added to his bill. He will stay three

---

[12] To cite a typical example of police supervision on the continent of Europe, every tourist in Boulogne-sur-Mer, France, must supply the following items of information : name, surname, birth date, birth place, nationality, profession, home address, identity papers, date of entry, place coming from and place going to.

[13] Alice Morse Earle, *Stage-Coach and Tavern Days* (New York, 1900), p. 4.

[14] Denniston, "Curbing the Souvenir Hunter," *Hotel Management* (May, 1922).

or four days. Finally the maid will report that his room was not slept in.

Yes, a lot of "souvenir hunters" stop with us, and I have known them to steal the silverware and towels—in fact most anything they could find loose. Not long ago a lady who had a baby and a baby carriage registered for a room. The next morning the maid reported everything in the room stolen, except the furniture. Pillows, pillow-cases, sheets, bedspread, woolen blankets, anything that could be piled into the baby cab had been taken.

We also find ourselves molested with "dead beats." Many of these carry a small battered suit case. After spending a few days with us they will leave the old grip in their rooms and we never see them again. They register fictitious names as a rule, so we are obliged to take the loss, which runs up into a good sum every year. We try our best to collect in advance, but unless it is a known fact that the person in question is a dead beat, people with baggage must be given credit.

Our hotel is molested at times with "four flushers." These are the least liked people with whom we come in contact. They are always trying to entertain and have everything charged to their rooms. They always carry a bank book, but if one accommodates them he will find their accounts short.[15]

According to a branch manager for the Burns Detective Agency, an international organization, hotel criminals are more plentiful in the United States than in any other country. While Grace Moore, the opera singer, was swimming with her husband at Miami, Florida, gems which had an estimated value of $81,000, were stolen from her hotel room. Police Chief Robert Teaney of Miami told the Associated Press, March 16, 1934, that the precious stones had been recovered by an arrest in New York City. Jewelry valued at more than $70,000, taken from another hotel room in this popular winter resort, had also been recovered at the

[15] Adapted from a paper prepared by the manager of a 150-room hotel in a small city.

same time. "In the wake of the very wealthy there invariably follows a train of blackmailers, jewel thieves, and other types of crooks, most of them clever and daring, who make the very rich the special object of their attention."[16]

Large hotels employ house detectives whose duty it is to guard the guests as well as the hotel. A night watchman collects keys that have been left in the doors. Since many hotel registers have been replaced by registration blanks, it is no longer possible for the crook to study the roster of guests. The credit department, doormen, desk clerks, bellboys, mail clerks and porters coöperate in watching guests who behave in ways that arouse suspicion. Ideally the entire personnel form a collective secret service department.[17]

In spite of this watchfulness some of the most intelligent gentlemen burglars "establish headquarters at a hotel and prey upon the city for months without being discovered." The name and atmosphere of a first-class hotel gives these well dressed criminals a seemingly honest front. In fact "hotel detective work requires more experience and skill than any other branch of criminal detection," according to the reported statement of a Milwaukee house officer.

A host of professional crooks travel about the country, living at the best hotels and preying upon the unsuspecting public. Bandits, burglars, blackmailers, forgers, confidence men, white slavers, dope sellers and bootleggers are included in the tribe of nomadic parasites.

Daring holdup men, operating from a good hotel, camouflage their activities by a pretension of legitimate business. They mingle with officers and employees of large firms. They obtain information concerning pay rolls and mail deliveries, strike quickly and make a well planned getaway.

The forger causes the hotel detective the greatest grief. Crooks

---

[16] *Chamber's Journal*, July, 1931, "Hotel Life As It Is and Was" by the manager of a luxury hotel.

[17] For ten rules to be used in preventing hotel thefts see William J. Stuart, "Tips From a Former Hotel Crook," *Hotel Management*, July, 1933.

have developed forgery to a greater art than any other crime. They prey not only upon the public, but they specialize in swindling hotels. The wool is often pulled over the eyes of the most suspicious hotel clerk. Credentials, local references, lines of credit, all of which seem bona fida, turn out to be fakes. The forger with a new bank roll and a new name has meanwhile sought new pastures.

Floor sneaks are undoubtedly among the cleverest of burglars. The victim's key is pushed out of the lock by a special pair of tweezers. The key falls on the carpet inside the room and does not wake the sleeping guest. Taking no chances, the sneak retreats to his own room for a time. He returns, opens the door noiselessly with a skeleton key, and while the guest sleeps on, makes off with money and valuables. The hotel usually makes good the loss sustained by the guest.[18]

The criminal racket, one of the most sinister developments in organized crime, strikes directly at particular industries. It has been defined as "a conspiracy operated in the field of business to control illegally prices, competition and employment, and to obtain protection from the enforcement of the law. The hotel field, dealing with the public from so many different angles, and requiring services from so many different lines is peculiarly exposed to the menace of rackets."[19]

MORAL HOLIDAYS

Canons of conduct are more or less absolute in the home community. Conformity to them is largely enforced by such

---

[18] "Hotel Detective Constantly Battling Smart Criminals," *The Hotel World*, March 3, 1923, p. 35. William Healy on p. 322 of *The Individual Delinquent* (Boston, 1915), describes a professional criminal who lived at first-class hotels. Jack Black, the reformed burglar, whose book *You Can't Win* (New York, 1926), is one of the most reliable of the criminal autobiographies, describes on p. 223 an experience while prowling through a hotel room: "Instead of putting my hand on a pair of pants, it touched something furry that came to life with a start and a growl, and fastened a pair of strong jaws on my forearm."

[19] Gordon L. Hostetter, "The Many Ways in Which the Racketeer Makes Inroads into Hotel Profits," *Hotel Management*, May, 1933, pp. 228-29.

spontaneous emotional gestures as the reproving tone or the scornful laugh. In the hotel the restraints of the face-to-face intimate groups are not present—unless, to be sure, one is traveling with a group—and the tendency under these circumstances is to follow impulses. Manners and morals must be thoroughly a part of the individual if they are to remain operative. They must be grounded in habit and not merely enforced by custom. It is because ideals have not been woven into the warp and woof of life-organization that "men and women, who in their own communities command respect, on going to a hotel, take a 'moral holiday'! "[20]

During an interview a man poked his head into the office, said "Hello" with the familiarity of an intimate and entered. "I want that room next door, a table, some chips and six chairs," he said. "Can't you come up? Bring somebody with you. The limit will be a dollar. We'll begin at eight and play till about twelve. And say," he added, winking at the interviewer. "Have you got a little sweet soda or ginger ale? Got a bottle in Toronto. Harder to get there than here. They tell me sweet soda is good to mix it with." After the arrangements were made the manager explained that the visitor was an old friend he had known in another hotel. "That's the way it is with a hotel man," he said. "You must accommodate your guests."

According to a veteran colored porter the hotel is the "worst gambling place in the world." "Boy, can you lead me to a little game?" was the frequent inquiry when he took a satchel. Hotel gambling is sometimes a very exciting affair, the winnings and losses running into the thousands of dollars. Such interest is perhaps due to the fact that gambling is a "fighting play." "There is charm of danger as such, enjoyment of bold betting, which, in the changing course of the game is constantly renewed."[21]

---

[20] See also pp. 5 and 6.
[21] Karl Groos, *The Play of Man* (New York, 1901), p. 213.

Hotels have always been associated with the selling of liquor. Firebaugh's *Inns of Greece and Rome* is as much a history of drinking and carousing as of hotels. The inns and taverns of Old England and of the American colonies were frequently more devoted to the sale of intoxicants than to the housing of travelers. In pre-Volsteadian days many New York "hotels" were merely saloons with a few rooms attached to give the legal rights of a hotel.[22]

In colonial times drinking at the village tavern was a widely accepted folkway and the landlord was an important personality in the village. With the growth of the temperance movement there came an increasing hostility toward the hotel man as well as toward the saloon-keeper. By the end of the nineteenth century, although still important in village politics, he was no longer a member of the small-town aristocracy. After the passing of the Eighteenth Amendment, however, he "regained the position and influence that were formerly his."[23]

Before prohibition practically all hotels had bars. Profits from the bar were so large that the manager frequently paid little attention to costs, judging the success of his business from the total profits over a long period. The Biltmore in New York City, for example, is said to have made two million dollars profit on its beverage business during the year before prohibition. Prior to the dry era there were no books on hotel management and no specialists in hotel accounting. Installation of cost systems usually revealed that the dining room and guest rooms were losing money. After prohibition many hotel managers had to reorganize their budgets en-

---

[22] The "Raines Law" of New York (1896) attempted to regulate the sale of alcoholic liquors by permitting Sunday drinking only in hotels. As a result saloons built bedrooms adjacent to their bars. There were 1,407 certified hotels in Manhattan and the Bronx alone, 1,160 of them created by the Raines Law. See Havelock Ellis, *The Task of Social Hygiene* (Boston and New York, 1912), chap. IX.

[23] Williamson, *op. cit.*, pp. 142-44.

tirely. This was a factor in the rising prices for hotel accommodations.

It was natural that an institution so long associated with drinking and the sale of liquors should experience a continuation of these practices during legal prohibition. In this respect hotels were analogous to immigrant communities, such as "Back of the Yards" in Chicago, where the folkway of drinking—which had been an accepted custom in the old country—tended to persist in spite of "governmental interference." Although it was usually only the cheap hotels that engaged directly in bootlegging, the managers of the best hostelries were not always successful in preventing their employees from selling liquor. After lining up the bellboys of a leading hotel in the lobby, a certain deputy sheriff went into an adjacent trunk room and reappeared soon with one hundred quarts of bonded liquor.[24]

During prohibition bottled beverages were commonly under the control of the head bellman and had no financial connection with the hotel. No doubt some people drink mineral water and ginger ale for their own merit as beverages. It is unlikely, however, that guests in a 175-room hotel would consume from fifty to two hundred bottles of these drinks daily for their sake alone.

Hotel men had other grievances against prohibition in addition to the loss of the bar and its income. They could discharge an employee for selling liquor but they could not prevent guests from bringing their own. The increasing frequency of wild parties made it necessary to enlarge the furniture replacement fund. Drinks might be mixed in a glass on the table and, as intoxication progressed, on the table cover. "They did not seem to know whether they were pouring into the glass or onto the table," complained the head housekeeper of an ultra-fashionable hotel. Generally, of course, the guest was made to pay for such destruction.

---

[24] *Seattle Daily Times,* July 25, 1929, p. 19.

One hotel preserves photographs of the interior of a room after a Princeton student, the son of a rich man, held a party there. Every breakable thing was smashed. Even the tiles and the plumbing fixtures in the bathroom were torn out.[25]

The hotel, like any other institution, has an outward appearance and an inner reality. The casual visitor sees only the structure, the service, the externalities. The personnel and the permanent guests see behind the scenes.

Wild parties are frequent in hotels. Guests do things they would never consider doing in the privacy of their own homes. I remember one time when the members of an orchestra occupied rooms above ours. For several days thay had a continuous party, banging drums and tooting saxophones in addition to using their vocal chords effectively. We finally had peace for a few days when they were evicted.

The bellhops are usually the go-betweens for the bootlegger and the hotel patron. The first thing many men do when they stop in a new hotel is to quiz the elevator boy or a bellhop about sources of supply. As one of the hops said to me, "If they look all right, we give it to 'em." Usually the bellhops do not peddle the booze, but for their services in recommending a certain phone number, they receive a commission which is a welcome supplement to their meager wage. They take long chances in giving information. If the manager should catch any of his employees selling or giving sources for liquor, he would immediately discharge the offender to protect himself.

Much furniture is broken up during liquor parties. I have seen chairs that had been smashed to kindling wood after a pair of husky inebriates had tossed them about. Beds are often broken

---

[25] Herbert Corey, "What the Hotel Men Think of Us," *Colliers*, February 14, 1925, p. 15. In answer to a query concerning the kinds of hotel property most frequently destroyed by guests, Seattle managers emphasized the damage done to bedding, furniture and carpets by burning tobacco, especially cigarettes. "After a banquet we know that fully half the table covers used will have burns in them from carelessly dropped cigars and cigarettes," writes Margaret A. Barnes, executive housekeeper at The Roosevelt in New York. ["How We Behave Away From Home," *American Magazine*, CXI (March, 1931), 150.]

by being jumped on. Wallpaper suffers from blotches of liquid. The hootch has been known to remove varnish from dressers and desks. Tumblers suffer more than their share, for the bathrooms have tile floors on which no tumbler can find a soft landing place.[26]

A young woman who worked for six months as assistant night clerk in an exclusive Canadian hostelry contrasts the behavior of Englishmen and Americans when drunk.

With the great majority of English people there is a definite opinion that being drunk in public or in the presence of women is simply "not done." Girls refuse to dance with a persistent offender and he is dropped by men because "he cannot carry his liquor like a gentleman." The Englishman, who had been on a stag party and had come in the worse for wear, was fearfully shy of asking me for his mail or key and would hang around until he could catch the eye of the male clerk. Even though an employee of the hotel I was a woman and he was ashamed to have me see him drunk.

The American in the same state, however, seemed to have no shame at all. He was usually one of the merely wealthy guests who had made money rather too late for it to improve their manners. He would come up to me and enter into long conversations, the tenor of them being, "I'm drunk, I'm damned drunk, and I don't give a damn who knows it." Then he would tell me how lonely he was and that all he needed was a little love or friendship. He was either maudlin or roaring drunk. When in the latter state concerted action on the part of any men around would carry him away from my vicinity.

Repeal has no doubt accentuated the up swing of the business cycle in the hotel industry. Beer and wines seem to whet the appetite and increase the food bills. People not only eat larger quantities, but they also spend more time doing it and get more enjoyment in the process. The be-

---

[26] From the hotel experience of a young man who had lived four years in a transient hotel.

havior after recent important football games, however, seems even wilder than similar hysteria during the prohibition era. Following a University of Washington victory over the University of Oregon at Portland, damages to the furnishings and equipment at one hotel were estimated at more than one thousand dollars.

Pitchers, glasses, bottles and even chairs were hurled from upper-story windows. In another hotel supporters of both universities held a water battle on one of the floors with fire hoses. At a third hostelry two rooters were seen perched on a two-foot ledge outside a fifth story window, cheering loudly in unintelligible terms.[27]

Then there is the problem of unmarried couples. Practically all hotels entertain them in varying numbers. The clerk in the most carefully regulated hostelry does not dare ask a couple for their marriage license unless they are intoxicated, make a disturbance, or are so young that it is very evident they are not married. The innocent guest would be highly offended and might sue the hotel for damages. Second and third-rate hotels often serve as convenient places for incognito and irregular sex relations. This is more or less taken for granted by the managers and, unless too obvious, is ignored.[28] Even at fashionable hotels old men sometimes register with their "daughters" or "grand-daughters." Some resort hotels become notorious as havens for the business man and his stenographer or the young bachelor and his "girl friend."

The couple registered under an assumed name. The girl had only a small traveling bag—no other luggage. The floor clerk eyed them closely. While they went to the theatre, the couple left the bag on the floor of their room. As an experiment they

---

[27] Adapted from the *University of Washington Daily*, October 16, 1934.
[28] For a discussion of hotels as vice resorts see Howard B. Woolston, *Prostitution in the United States* (New York, 1921), pp. 141-43 and 237-38.

marked its location with pins. When they returned the bag had been moved and there was a mark on the bed where it had been placed. Shortly afterwards the house detective came to the door. "Traveling rather light, aren't you?" he said. Then he simply asked for payment in advance.

Hotel men in port cities deprecate the explosive behavior of sailors on shore leave. Six men of the sea with their partners once formed a party lasting three days. The hotel put up with them merely because the management needed the money. "Arbuckle parties" are, of course, not limited to any particular occupation or economic class. Frequently they are very disturbing to other hotel guests.

Several times I have been greatly disturbed by neighbors who made the night hideous and sleepless for me by their carousing. Undoubtedly booze figured largely in such parties, and sometimes questionable women guests, of whom I was forced to complain. Even decent hotels hesitated to turn out these well-paying roomers, who often came from families who would be scandalized to discover how their sons abused the freedom of hotels. Friends of mine have had similar experiences with their hotel neighbors.[29]

The assistant manager in a large San Francisco hotel, a man who has "worked up from the bells" and has always had the detective side of the management, states that the prostitute "can't be detected as easily now as twenty years ago. If the house officer at that time were to have gone to sleep, like Rip Van Winkle, he would have awakened to a very different situation. It used to be easy, but now you can not tell." He pooh-poohs the manager who says that he can pick out the people who are not married.

At times women of disrepute get into our hotel. One would think when they arrive and approach the desk that they were

---

[29] By the woman who had lived for brief periods in about five hundred hotels.

the most innocent of women. The only way to find out about them is to watch closely. When found to be positively wrong they are at once requested to leave. Some will accept this request in a most ladylike manner; others will abuse you to the utmost.[30]

During the prohibition era the Supreme Court held that it was up to the hotel man to know if his bellboys were procurers or bootleggers. This was undoubtedly a difficult task, particularly if he was head of a chain of six or eight hotels. Some of these hotel men had friends, however, who, on their trips around the country tried out hotel employees by attempting to bribe them into buying liquor or bringing "girls" into the hotel. One of these men had the following experience.

He registered under an assumed name, posing as a commercial traveler. He sent the bellboy on a trivial errand to the drug store and gave him a dollar tip. Then he tried to get into conversation with him, but this failed since the hotel had taught its bellboys what to say in response to questions. He tried to get the "kid" to bootleg and bring in a "girl," but the boy would not do it. The next morning he talked to the manager, whom he knew well, and found that his endeavors had been reported. He also learned that eight employees had been dismissed during the previous week for susceptibility to just such temptations.

In one of the large Loop hotels of Chicago a transient frequently tips a telephone girl four or five successive times, and then tries to make a "date." This is such a common practice that the girls expect it and, when a man tips them, jokingly predict the time when he will ask for a "date."

"Tourists Accommodated—and No Questions Asked!" the title of a leading article in *Hotel Management*,[31] illustrates one

---

[30] From the paper by a Wisconsin hotel man.
[31] October, 1929.

type of criticism that hotel men are making of "accommodation houses and cabin developments." That unmarried
guests and noisy patrons are frequently entertained by auto
camps is no doubt as true as in the case of many so-called
"legitimate" hotels. In the better cottage courts, however,
the guest must not only register his name and address, as in
a hotel, but also the license number of his car. Completeness
of registration is often an index to the moral character of a
camp. When asked why he did not include names in the
registration the proprietor of a resort camp said, "I used to
include the names, but the people kicked too much. Too
many men come here with other men's wives." The fact
that 31 out of 96 auto camps in the vicinity of Seattle do
not require registration is very significant.

Souvenir hunting does not appear to be as common in
the auto courts of the Pacific Coast as in the hotels. The
owner of an Oregon camp declared that, although the court
had been established four years, "we have never had a thing
stolen, but have returned hundreds of articles including a
wrist watch, a diamond ring, and one hundred dollars in
cash." At almost all camps, however, it is the rule to pay in
advance. "That's the only way to run an auto camp," one
of the managers asserted.

In the West honesty still prevails, and when one stays at a
tourist court one does not bother to lock things up. Farther east
the owners have to be a little more on guard against their guests,
and the guests against one another. Cottage linen disappears
regularly, even if heavily stenciled with the name of U Pop Inn
or Gibson's Homey Homes.

And up and down the land, especially outside the cities, women
who are still too respectable to sign a fake name on a hotel register drive out with temporary mates and enjoy a lawless privacy.
The lowlier cottage camps ask no questions and take in a huge
love-nest income; the better camps are increasingly more care-

ful and require their guests to sign in the guest book, giving the license number of their car. Ordinances and laws have as yet not gone far beyond sanitary regulations.[32]

It is evident, therefore, that hotel life has a pathological aspect. It encourages individuation, i.e. the free play of impulses when released from restraint. Stealing and immoral behavior are simply manifestations of this decadence in tradition. They are commonly associated with the freedom and detachment of a mobile existence. Conventional behavior must be well integrated to be effective. These moral holidays of the hotel environment dramatize a widespread disintegration of the mores which is occurring under the influence of metropolitan life. Mobility has always been associated with disorganization. In fact "the word 'traveler' in medieval England was used in popular discourse to designate the thief."[33] Because of this relationship it is significant that metropolites "live in flats and flit from flat to flat." Even those who do not make their homes in habitats for travelers are coming more and more to live like hotel dwellers.

[32] McCarthy and Littell, "Three Hundred Thousand Shacks," *Harper's Magazine*, CLXVII (July, 1933), 187-88. Quoted by permission of *Harper's Magazine*.

[33] Edwin H. Sutherland, *Principles of Criminology* (Chicago and Philadelphia, 1934), p. 73.

CHAPTER XII

THE HOTEL AND AMERICAN SOCIETY

LIFE IN the great city differs fundamentally from that in the isolated village community. A native of the provincial hamlet is known in all the relations of his life. "Everyone knows everything about everyone else." The metropolite, however, is generally known in but one or two aspects of his personality. For him physical proximity and social distance is the common experience.

A very large part of the population of great cities, including those who make their homes in tenements and apartment houses, live much as people do in some great hotel, meeting but not knowing one another. The effect of this is to substitute fortuitous and casual relationships for the more intimate and permanent associations of the smaller community. It is probably the breaking down of local attachments and the weakening of the restraints and inhibitions of the primary group under the urban environment, which are largely responsible for the increase of vice and crime in great cities.[1]

William Dean Howells in *The Rise of Silas Lapham* speaks of people on the Boston Commons embracing "as if they were in the privacy of a railway car." The absolute standards and insistence on conformity characteristic of the American village of fifty years ago did not tolerate metropolitan phenomena of this kind. Under the influence of steam and electric railways, the automobile, the telephone, rural free

---

[1] See the article of Robert E. Park, "The City," *American Journal of Sociology*, XX (March, 1915), 607-8 and 595. "By primary groups I mean those characterized by intimate face-to-face association and coöperation," [Charles Horton Cooley, *Social Organization* (New York, 1909), p. 23.]

delivery and the radio, however, small towns and even open country communities are becoming urbanized. These modern means of transportation and communication permit the farmer to make contacts on the basis of his interests. They have, in other words, made possible a partial emancipation from the tyranny of local gossip.

In a big hotel this urbanity is accentuated. Status is largely a pecuniary matter. Fads and fashions arise and are copied by less successful admirers. There is novelty, excitement and uniqueness. The prosaic and uninteresting make no impression. Glitter and dazzle dominate.

Nobody bothers about anyone else. Everyone is alone with himself. The events that happen do not constitute entire human destinies complete and rounded off. They are fragments merely, scraps, pieces. . . . A glance that travels up does not reach the eyes. It stops at one's clothes.[2]

In colonial times the reputation of an inn depended largely on the personality of the landlord and the skill of his cook. Today the hotel manager is a business executive and the only way his personality can be expressed is in the service and appointments of his hotel. The twentieth century hostelry is a great efficient device for providing transient guests with bed and board. It serves that "important percentage of mankind that travels from place to place seeking new fields to conquer, developing new markets, enlarging commerce and benefiting industry."[3]

"The rage for mechanical devices may be the ruin of a once good hotel; for the basis of righteousness in a hotel is not mechanical devices but personal human contacts," wrote Arnold Bennett about European hotels. "If you complained of the coffee's being cold," he continues, "you were re-

---

[2] Baum, *op. cit.*, pp. 237 and 299.
[3] From a pamphlet by W. I. Hamilton.

minded : 'Ah! But you can bolt your door while in bed.' "[4]
His criticism applies with even more force to the standard-
ized hospitality in the larger and more impersonal hotels of
America.

Hotels and travel are closely related, for the hotel is a
business institution that caters to the traveler. All hostelries,
in fact, house transient guests. Otherwise they are not hotels.
Even the so-called "permanents" need remain only a month
to acquire that name. Compared with the area in which
the hotel is located its population is always relatively transient. People come and go. There is an air of impermanence
—"just a place to hang one's hat." It is natural, therefore,
that an intimate bond should exist between hotels and transportation. Caravansery, coaching inn, commercial hotel and
cottage court have developed in response to the needs of
travelers by caravan, stage-coach, railroad and automobile,
respectively. The large number, the variety and the wide
geographical distribution of habitats for travelers in the
United States are indices to the restlessness and mobility of
the American people.

Many of these American tourists are merely being trans-
ported. "Travelers returning from a summer's tour of Alaska
often speak more enthusiastically of the double helpings of
apple pie at a small hotel in Skagway than of the splendid
scenery they saw."[5] Even if the scenery did impress them, intelligent travel is something more than seeing sights. It involves learning new ways of living.

"Homes are becoming more hotel-like," the hotel men say,
and they are thinking of the way in which hotels have pioneered in such things as bathtubs, modern heating arrange-

[4] Bennett, "Private Thoughts on European Hotels," *The Bookman* (December, 1926).

[5] Barnes, "How We Behave Away From Home," *The American Magazine*,
CXI (March, 1931).

ments, and comfortable beds. Travelers have become acquainted with these "new fangled notions" in hotels and have gradually introduced them in their own domiciles. But the American home is also coming to be more and more of a "hotel home," psychologically speaking. In addition to new creature comforts American families are acquiring new ways of behaving. Like the emancipated couples of the hotel world, a growing number of urbanized families are small, mobile and loosely integrated. The divergence of interests in these families is suggested by the extent to which the members scatter in the course of their daily or weekly activities.

The father is away on business, the mother is at work or engaged among her many outside interests, and the children are at school, the club, the dance, or the movies. The "common" meals are common no longer ; breakfast comes for each one when he is ready, and luncheon is found elsewhere. Even summer vacation, if there is one, finds the family separated. The summer camp or summer work takes some of the children, while the parents may go away for a "change of scenery."[6]

One result of this "trend toward hotel living"—in the psychological use of that phrase—is that an increasing number of children are learning the independent ways of the hotel child. Another is a divorce rate in the United States more than five times as great as it was in 1870. This rate is higher, in fact, than in any other country except Russia.

In large cities the individual home, with its numerous activities and relative permanence, is obviously passing. With the exception of a temporary check during the depression, the trend is definitely toward multiple dwellings, wholesale housekeeping and decline in the number and variety of activities carried on in the home. Hotels and tourist habitats are increasing both in number and in size. Americans are

[6] Jerome Davis in a paragraph on "the hotel home" in Jerome Davis and H. E. Barnes, *An Introduction to Sociology* (Boston and New York, 1927), p. 717.

coming more and more to use the apartment house and hotel as places of abode. The increase in residential hotels is particularly significant because it represents a situation in which the hitherto stable and organized home becomes amalgamated with the impersonal and efficient but frequently disorganizing inn. The individual members of the hotel family are quite free to follow their wishes, it is true, but there is danger that this release from restraints may disintegrate the group.

"Have you ever lived in Europe or in any foreign country?" asks a hotel child. "Did you take part where you lived in the life around you? Or did you just live in your hotel and see the sights? That is the trouble with people who live abroad all their lives; they have no roots; they don't belong to anything. And that is the way with people like me who live in a hotel always; we are in a certain degree like people who are living in a foreign country."[7]

The hotel population is essentially an aggregation of such displaced individual units. There is physical nearness, but social farness. Tipping is an index to this distance, for we do not tip our equals. Here are the ants and the aphids. The Gold Coast and Back of the Yards meet in a hotel, perhaps, but the relation is symbiotic rather than social. There is a tremendous difference in wealth and social status between the luxuriously gowned woman of leisure and the isolated immigrant maid who does her room. The extremes of American society are to be seen in a big hotel.

The metropolitan hotel is a social center, to be sure, but for the larger community—and that is different. Contacts are usually anonymous and casual. If a person wants sociability he must bring it with him. It has been suggested that the worst hell is not a place where people hate you but where they are merely indifferent. If this be true the lobby of a big hotel would make a good inferno.

[7] "The True Story of a Hotel Child," *The Designer*, April, 1922.

18

If there were anything in the instinct of gregariousness as it is ordinarily interpreted, one ought to feel particularly comfortable and enlivened in a hotel lobby. Actually it is probably the most dreary place on earth.[8]

Exaggerated statements about urban life become realities in the hotel environment. Metropolitan problems exhibit themselves in accentuated form. The general significance, then, of hotel life is the light it throws on human behavior in what Graham Wallas has called the Great Society. The detachment, freedom, loneliness and release from restraints that mark the hotel population are only to a lesser degree characteristic of modern life as a whole. The hotel is, in fact, a symbol of changes that are taking place not only in the manners and morals of American society, but wherever the influence of machine industry is felt.

---

[8] From the university professor who had "traveled a good deal but never learned to enjoy life in a hotel."

SELECTED BIBLIOGRAPHY

Anderson, Nels, *The Hobo: The Sociology of the Homeless Man* (chap. 3, "The Lodging-House: The Homeless Man at Home"), Chicago, 1923.

Baum, Vicki, *Grand Hotel*. New York, 1931. A novel dramatizing the impersonality and detachment of hotel life.

Bennett, Arnold, *Imperial Palace*, London, 1930. A work of fiction describing the management problems of a big luxury hotel.

Boomer, Lucius M., *Hotel Management: Principles and Practice*, Second edition, New York, 1931. The best book of its kind in English. Contains bibliography.

Cole, H. E., *Stage Coach and Tavern Tales of the Old Northwest*, 1930. Pictures of American taverns during the period from 1830 to 1860.

Encyclopedia of the Social Sciences, articles on "Hospitality," "Hotels," and "Lodging Houses."

Ferguson, Melville F., *Motor Camping on Western Trails*, New York, 1925. The story of an automobile tour in 1922 and 1923. No-camp, free-camp and pay-camp belts in the United States are differentiated (pp. 58-59).

Firebaugh, W. C., *The Inns of Greece and Rome and a History of Hospitality from the Dawn of Time to the Middle Ages*, Chicago, 1923. Not well organized, but uses numerous quotations from documents.

Gautier, Marcel, *L'Hotellerie: Etude Theorique et Pratique*, Paris, 1932. A study of tourism and the hotel industry. Contains bibliography.

Glücksmann, Robert, *Das Gaststättenwesen*, Stuttgart, 1927. The most scholarly German work on hotel administration. Includes interesting historical material.

Hamilton, W. I., *Promoting New Hotels: When does It Pay?*, New York, 1930. Includes charts showing trends in the hotel industry.

Jenkins, Stephen, *The Old Boston Post Road*, New York, 1913. Two hundred illustrations and maps.

Lewis, Sinclair, *Work of Art*, New York, 1934. A novel describing from the standpoint of the manager many different types of American hotels.

Ludy, Robert B., *Historic Hotels of the World: Past and Present*, Philadelphia, 1927. One hundred and thirty-two illustrations. Although the emphasis in this book is on concrete unique events connected with "historic" or leading hotels, occasional sentences or paragraphs make significant generalizations.

Maskell, Henry P. and Gregory, Edward W., *Old Country Inns of England*, London, 1912. "We have attempted a classification and description of the inns which not only sheltered our forefathers when on their journeys, but served as their usual places for meeting and recreation."

McKenzie, R. D., *The Metropolitan Community*, New York, 1933. Fig. 32 on p. 246 shows the age-sex composition of the population in different types of hotels.

Mead, William, *The Grand Tour in the Eighteenth Century*, Boston, 1914. "Our main theme is the touring of Englishmen upon the Continent of Europe in the eighteenth century." Includes bibliographical note.

Ogilvie, F. W., *The Tourist Movement: An Economic Study*, London, 1933.

Park, Robert E. and Burgess, Ernest W., *Introduction to the Science of Sociology* (chap. 5, "Social Contacts"), Chicago, 1931.

Sarkies, E. L., *The Importance of the Hotel Industry*, Leiden, Holland, 1933. A doctoral dissertation at the *Rijksuniversiteit te Leiden*. Includes interesting historical material and a twenty-seven-page bibliography.

Taylor, Bayard, *Views A-Foot; or Europe Seen With Knapsack and Staff*, Twentieth edition, revised, New York, 1855. Observations on European travel ninety years ago.

United States Department of Commerce, Bureau of the Census, *Census of Hotels*, 1930.

Willey, Malcolm M. and Rice, Stuart A., *Communication Agencies and Social Life* (chap. 6, "Touring and Travel"), New York, 1933. A Recent Social Trends monograph.

Williamson, Jefferson, *The American Hotel: An Anecdotal History*, New York, 1930. The best source available on the history of American hotels.

Wolfe, A. B., *The Lodging House Problem in Boston*, Boston, 1906.

Zorbaugh, Harvey W., *The Gold Coast and the Slum: A Sociological Study of Chicago's Near North Side* (chap. 4, "The World of Furnished Rooms"), Chicago, 1929.

INDEX

Actor, 93, 97-98; little "actor," 119
Actor's hotel, 97
Ahrens Publications, 63
Airplane, 91
Alaska, 179
Alsace, 90, 91
Ambrose, Clinton A., 25
American Automobile Association, 79, 141
American hotel as a social center, 144-53
American hotel lobbies, public nature of, 145
Amsterdam, 88, 89
Ancient Greece, 139
Anderson, Nels, 29, 183
Apartment hotel differentiated, 63-65
Apartment house, 5, 50, 52, 63, 64, 67, 70, 71, 73, 74, 84, 87, 100, 102, 104, 107, 122, 177, 181
Argentina, people like to travel, 90
Asia, 17, 18
Ask-Mr.-Foster office, 42
Athens, Greece, 12
Atlantic City, 135
Atlantic Coast, 82
Ausfluge, 91
Australia, 14, 94
Austria, 19, 41, 42, 43, 57, 90, 142, 143, 144; people prefer to act as hosts, 90
Austro-Hungarian Empire, 40, 41
Auto camp. *See* Tourist camp
Automobile, 8, 24, 25, 38, 50, 53, 79-80, 91, 95, 97, 99, 127, 136-39, 141-44, 152, 153, 177, 179, 183

Bad Ischl, 41

Bagman, 94, 96
Balkan States, 42
Baltimore, 20; guest rooms per 1,000 population, 84n
Barnes, H. E., 180n
Barnes, Margaret A., 170n, 179n
Baum, Vicki, 5n, 178n, 183
Bavaria, 43, 91, 94, 144
Beard, Miriam, 53n
Belgium, 44
Bellboy, 1, 27, 119, 120, 123, 129, 155, 156-57, 165, 169, 170, 174
Bennett, Arnold, 58, 157, 178-79, 183
Berlin, 32, 44-45, 87, 91; "Centrum," 32; Unter den Linden, 32, 44; "Zoo," 32
Bicycle, 19, 142, 143
Biltmore Hotel, New York, 168
Black, Jack, 166n
Blackstone Hotel, 111, 161
Boarding house, 8, 55-56, 61, 88, 99
Boomer, Lucius M., 64n, 183
Bootlegging, 169, 170
Boston, 20, 21, 22, 31; Commons, 177; guest rooms per 1,000 population, 83n
Boulogne-sur-Mer, France, 163n
Bowery, 30
Bremerton, Washington, 37
Bridal couples, 149
British Columbia, 25
Brooks, Lee M., 139n
Budapest, 57, 88
Buffalo, guest rooms per 1,000 population, 83n
Bulgaria, 42
Bull and Mouth, 19
Bungalows, 18
Burgess, Ernest W., 102n, 116n, 153n, 158n, 184